PELTIER GLASS TOY MARBLES

An American Legend

Sami Arim, Mike Johnson & Gino Biffany

© 2016 by Sami Arim

All rights reserved. No part of this work may be reproduced or used in any form or by any means - graphic, electronic, or mechanical, including photocopying or information storage and retrieval systems—without written permission from the publisher.
The scanning, uploading and distribution of this book or any part thereof via the Internet or via any other means without the permission of the publisher is illegal and punishable by law. Please purchase only autorized editions and do not participate in or enchorage the electronic piracy of copyrighted materials.

Book Design by: Dee Turman (www.dturmanillustration.com)

ISBN 978-0-692-77782-4

Printed In China

TABLE OF CONTENTS

1. INTRODUCTION 7
2. THE PELTIER GLASS COMPANY HISTORY 13
3. EARLY PRODUCTION.. 23
4. MILLER SWIRLS 29
5. THREE COLOR NATIONAL LINE RAINBOS 47
6. TWO COLOR NATIONAL LINE RAINBOS 65
7. MULTICOLOR SWIRLS 79
8. COMICS & ADVERTISING 85
9. RARITIES 101
10. TRANSPARENT & TRANSLUCENT NLRS............... 117
11. AVENTURINE 139
12. YING YANG PATTERN 153
13. SLAGS... 161
14. ORIGINAL PACKAGING....................................... 165
15. CONCLUSION.. 217
16. AUTHOR'S BIOGRAPHY...................................... 219

Acknowledgments

I would like to express gratitude to the following people who helped making this book a reality through with sharing knowledge and their collections, positive comments and encouragement, mentoring, support throughout the work and above all, their friendship.

In no particular order:
Chuck Garrett, Bill Bass, Kevin Plummer, Jamie Kummer, Larry & Cathy Svacina, Bill Tite, Mark & Dana Forrester, Chad Kline, Charles Williams, Jeff Wichmann, Clyde Tuller, Marty Ruhland, Bob Hutchisson, Jamie Browder, Hansel de Souza, Galen Wilcox, Steve Gorin, Landon Daniel, Ernie & Danie Kirk, Eddie Schubert

Front Page: A 11/16" Peltier Glass "Green Submarine" National Line Rainbo swirl.

Back Page Top: An 11/16" early Peltier Glass bronze & green aventurine on light green base glass. Heavy usage of aventurine points to earlier period as the aventurine usage declined as production moved to later Rainbos.

Back Page Bottom: A 13/16" Peltier Glass Miller swirl "Christmas Tree" with a magnificent pattern.

Sami Arim Contact info:
samiarim@yahoo.com Tel: 925 899 9261

Jamie Browder Contact info:
PO Box 4011, Peoria IL 61607 Tel: 309 697 2118

In Memory Of
Clyde Tuller, Gino Biffany, Norm Brown, & John Kinstler

This Book Is Dedicated To
My wife Luciana, my son Antonio and my daughter Ayla

1- INTRODUCTION

INTRODUCTION

    Playing marbles dates back to as long as people have been around. For centuries, children have loved these small round objects that they could roll on the ground and play and compete with. When marbles first made their way into a child's everyday life no one really knows. The earliest known production of glass can be traced back to 3500 B.C. in Mesopotamia. Making marbles from glass is another question that archeologists are still researching today. Marbles were made in ancient times from clay, rocks and materials that the everyday person had the means to work with. These small circular rocks or clay objects were eventually colored with dyes, hand painted or done in a fashion to make them more attractive to children.

    Handmade glass marbles go back to the early to mid-19th century. These marbles were handmade in Europe, mainly in Germany, but one can ascertain that they were also made in other parts of the world just from examining the different kinds of marbles that exist today. Handmade marbles from Europe were made in many sizes and their designs were limited only to the creators' imagination. The sizes ranged from a half inch or smaller to as large as 2-1/2". There are actually larger antique handmade marbles bigger than 2-1/2", but these are very rare. Collectors and historians still debate the purpose of these extraordinarily large marbles. Were they made for a store display, or for adults' to decorate their home? We may never know. It was probably for a myriad of reasons and it's likely they were simply expressions of early glass blowers willingness to showcase their talents to produce their best marble. During the time, they would be probably too large for children to play with, but then again, anything is possible. In the early days the marbles were made with more attention to detail, quality and colors. Pontils (discussed later in the book) were more carefully ground or polished and the overall presentation still captivates the marble collectors of today. This was probably because early production did not have the time constraints of the marbles to come. Eventually marble production was looked at as

1- INTRODUCTION

a business and the more marbles produced the better. As production moved towards the 20th century, the Second Industrial Revolution started catching up. Production had to move faster, more marbles had to be made in a day and as a result quality had to be compromised. New techniques were developed to produce more marbles and new equipment was invented. With new and improved production techniques, machines took the place of workers thereby maximizing their efforts. Toy marble makers had to make a profit to stay in business. American companies like MFChristensen, Akro Agate, Christensen Agate, Alley Agate and Peltier Glass were competing to produce more attractive marbles for kids to buy, play and collect. Companies now were making marbles in more reasonable sizes, generally half-inch and 5/8" which would easily fit in a child's hand. Larger marbles were also made, often referred to as "shooters", but the bulk of production was aimed at children and the fancier the marble the more popular they became. Most of the important marble making machines were developed in the early 20th century but the earliest recorded mass produced marbles began much earlier.

Mass production became possible in 1884, when Sam Dyke of Akron, Ohio, created a wooden block with six grooves, each of which held a lump of clay. An operator would roll a wooden paddle over all the clay balls at once, with a back-and-forth and slightly lateral motion, creating six marbles. With around 350 employees, Dyke's factory was cranking out five train carloads or about one million marbles every day. Mass production made marbles much cheaper to make, allowing the price to drop from about one penny each to a bag of 30 marbles for the same price. Other businessmen jumped on the bandwagon and Akron, Ohio soon became the marble capital of the late-19th century America.

In 1915, mass production of glass marbles began thanks to a revolutionary new machine invented by Akron's M.F. Christensen. His machine consisted of a screw conveyor made up of two grooved cylinders spun next to each other. A "slug" of molten glass was placed between the cylinders on one end and it was gradually carried down to the opposite side, simultaneously cooled and shaped into a sphere by the rolling grooves. The design worked so well, it has remained essentially unchanged and is still the most common way to make marbles today.

Making handmade marbles was fast becoming a part of history. Early machines to make marbles involved skilled labor. Workers in factories still had to manually feed the equipment to produce marbles. This period is referred to as the "Transitional Period" and the marbles were thus called

1- INTRODUCTION

Transitional marbles. They were in fact made by both hand and machine; a 50/50 division of labor and machinery. By the early 1920's, equipment was improved to minimize labor and thereby maximizing marble production. Finally, production could now be increased while overhead went down, in essence a new industry had begun and the potential for making money was not lost on a number of these early marble making pioneers.

When Peltier Glass decided to enter the toy marble making business, they were already an established, high quality glass producer. Having such an advantage with glass far ahead of their competitors, Peltier created unique innovations with their machinery. Peltier began producing what many consider today some of the most colorful marbles of their era. During the 1920's and 30's, the United States and Europe was beginning to enjoy a new era of design and colorful expression, a period of time now referred to as the Art Deco movement. The new Deco period took the place of the Art Nouveau period with an influential visual arts design style which first appeared in France after World War I. It flourished internationally in the 1930's and 1940's before its popularity waned after World War II. It was an eclectic style that combined traditional craft motifs with machine age imagery and materials. The style is often characterized by rich colors, bold geometric shapes, and lavish ornamentation. What better exemplified this movement than marbles? When one examines the products Peltier was making at the time, it was apparent that all the attributes of the Art Deco movement could easily be applied to early Peltier Glass as well. Other companies such as Akro Agate and Christensen Agate marbles of late 20's and 30's also began to ramp up production.

Whether modern or classic, the purpose of this book is to document the history and types of the marbles that were produced as toys for children that have become a collectible fascination for adults. The equipment and the type of glass used to make these early marbles are no longer available today. Glass production laws, regulations and restrictions changed the chemistry of the glass, and toy marbles are made with a different type of glass as well as more modern equipment in other countries outside of the United States. The Cats Eye marbles produced in Japan was the final straw. By producing a great looking marble with ease, it was almost impossible for competitors to keep up with them. Almost any collection today usually has a number of these colorful marbles named for their similarity to a cat's eye. Today, only two

1- INTRODUCTION

marble companies produce marbles in the United States. They are Jabo Inc. in Reno, Ohio, and Marble King, in Paden City, West Virginia. The world's largest manufacturer of playing marbles today is Vacor de Mexico (Fabricas Selectas). They produce over 90% of the world's marbles.

Peltier toy marble collectors affectionately give names to the marbles from the company. For some reason the names have stuck to the marbles and are part of the whole collecting folklore today. Names like Christmas Tree, Liberty, Rebel, Golden Rebel and many more are known and used on a daily basis in conversations, internet communications, online auction listings, etc. It is not really known when these names started being used by collectors. Peltier's original packaging did not use these names on their packaging cover. So it would be safe to assume that children started using the names as early as the time they were produced. New names entered into the collecting arena on a daily bases too. Collectors continue to discover marbles that are unique, early and rare examples. Enthusiastic collectors give fresh names to these marbles adding more into the mix every day. Some early names such as Wasp, Tiger, Bumble Bee, or Flaming Dragon will be extensively used in this book. Many new names, specifically if they represent a larger family or classification, will also be introduced with pictures and descriptions. However, it is not the intention or the task of this book to concentrate on too many new names that will confuse and muddy the waters for the current and future collectors. The use of names is kept minimal but descriptions of the marble's construction are given the utmost attention for readers to understand what to look for when they see a Peltier marble.

Peltier Glass toy marble production is a part of the past, but it will also always be part of the future as well. It documents an American pastime as good as it gets; a true collectible in every sense of the word. Peltier marbles are a research topic for not only historians of American glass, but also a passionate collectible for those who love and collect them. With this book becoming a reality, it is a testament to the timeless history of marbles, a product made for children to play with and a growing fascination for a generation of collectors entering the field of marble collecting today. More and more of these unique and beautiful marbles are disappearing from the antique dealer's shelves as rarer examples are already becoming part of collections that will not be available for future generations to see. By writing this book, we hope the resulting documentation of the history of marble and specifically Peltier marble production in America, will be shared by future generations to come.

1- INTRODUCTION

HOW ONE MARBLE GOT ITS NAME

There were many kids in the Ottawa Illinois School District. However, there was only one 17 year old, Mark Wiebe. He was a stand out in the classes, he had many friends and acquantances. He was an all around American young man. One of the things that was on his mind was his love for marbles. He lived marbles! The other thing that was on his mind was Type 1 Spinal Muscular Atrophy, as he had this incurable sickness. Forced to a wheel chair, his life was confined to a fraction of what his friends were able to do. Often his friends would come over and watch a movie, or talk about computers and listen to him talk about marbles. Mark's collection contained primarily Peltier, as they were easily found in his hometown of Ottawa. When he would find one that he didn't have, he was filled with joy. There were two outstanding men in Ottawa, who took him under their wings and worked with him on his collection. One in particular would help him identify his marbles and in general spend many hours with him while they discussed his most prized possession.

One of these men was none other then the well known Peltier collector Gino Biffany, who has a wealth of knowledge in the history of the Peltier Glass Company. The other was Boyce Lundstrom, one of the new owners of the Peltier Glass Company, who had a great interest in marbles. Between the two they kept Mark in a steady flow of marbles and valuable info on the Peltier marbles in general.

One day while Gino was over to Mark's house, Mark showed a marble to Gino thinking that it was a "Zebra". Gino mentioned to him that it really wasn't a "Zebra", as the "Zebra" was black ribbons on a white base and this particular marble had white ribbons on a black base and Gino told him that the marble in mention had no name and that Mark should name it. Mark thought on it for a couple of days and called Gino, telling him he had a name for it and that name was "Panda". Gino stated that was a good choice. Later, Gino contacted another well known marble collector Alan Bassinet and asked him if he would post this newly named marble on his Peltier identification page, giving it this new name. Alan immediately did and this is the story of how one marble got its name.

During the Amana show the same spring Gino got a phone call that Mark had passed away.

At the visitation services Mark's family brought Mark's beloved marbles to the funeral home, where they were displayed for all to see. His marbles were close to him in death as they were in life.

1- INTRODUCTION

Five of Mark's friends in school had been planning a trip to overseas to England and Ireland. Mark thought that was so neat to take such trip and see all of the sights himself, but couldn't because of his condition. He loved the movie "Braveheart" and the countryside that he saw. 24 hours before his friends departed, they got the news of Mark's death. One of the five kids leaving for overseas thought how emblematical it would be to take a bag of Mark's marbles with them and while on this trip they got the idea to leave some of Mark's marbles along the way. One of them rolled a marble through the gates of Buckingham Palace; they dropped another in the Atlantic ocean from Irelands cliffs of Moher; a third marble was tucked into a dark corner of the Beaumaris Castle in Whales; while yet another one was left in Dublin's famed St. Patricks Cathedral.

Mark has truly left his mark here on earth and in the minds of those that he reached out to.

Mark will be missed by his friend and others.

The story by Guy Gregg

THE PELTIER GLASS COMPANY HISTORY

Victor J. Peltier immigrated to the United States in 1859 at the age of 26. It remains unclear as to why he left his native Lorraine, France, but it was a fortunate event for the U.S. Glass industry. Young Victor had learned the art of glass-blowing from his father who had been in the business.

Victor spent twenty years in the glass business in New York before moving to Pennsylvania and then Iowa. He settled in Ottawa, Illinois in 1882 where he secured employment in one of the glass factories then in operation in that city. This was the Ottawa Flint Glass and Bottle Company. In 1886 this company closed down leaving Peltier jobless and with a large family to feed. In that same year he started his own glass business which he named the Novelty Glass Works.

Peltier experimented with the glass chemistry and composition and developed stained and opalescent flat glass comparable to those available from Europe.

Victor Peltier passed away in June 1911 and two sons Joseph and Sellers took over the business and expanded the company output to include new lines, but continued the manufacture of stained and opalescent glass as well.

As the 20th Century entered its second decade, it became evident that Peltier's company was a succesful one. The Community Business Review (an Ottawa journal) reported in the April 18, 1969 issue that in those early days the company's stained glass for church and business windows was very popular. Contracts from Ford Motor Corporation, Chrysler Corporation and the many companies that later became General Motors, to produce lenses for headlamps, relfectors, license plate light covers and ornate gearshift knobs were a big source of business for the Novelty Glass Works.

A business relationship had previosly been cultivated between Victor Peltier and Louis Comfort Tiffany whereby the later purchased a significant amount of colored glass for use in his famous lamps and other leaded glass art works. This, combined with the production of industrial glass and contracts to produce hobnailed candle holders and ashtrays helped the company thrive.

2-THE PELTIER GLASS COMPANY HISTORY

Above: An example of Tiffany lamp.

During and after the First World War sheets glass for the railroad cars manufactured by the Pullman Company was added to production.

In 1919 a disastrous fire demolished most of the Peltier plant at a loss figured at $150,000. The responding fire company was able to save the family mansion which stood only several hundred feet away. The local newspaper carried an article about the fire in which Sellers Peltier stated "Very little of the loss could be covered by insurance policies". He further stated that plans were already under way to rebuild the factory as soon as possible.

The factory was, of course, rebuilt and holding true to the tradition of many family owned businesses in the United States. The company name changed to "The Peltier Glass Company".

A mural in the present Peltier Glass Company building features pictures of the founding Peltier family and examples of the company production through the decades. Interesting too, from the vantage point of this volume, is that a representation of a marble machine created by Peltier workers is also shown. So it goes that Joseph and Sellers Peltier, the second generation owners, converted part of their plant to the production of toy glass marbles. This production expanded during the era of the Great Depression when stained sheet glass went out of fashion as a major building material.

It all began August 18, 1924 with an agreement between Milton H.

2-THE PELTIER GLASS COMPANY HISTORY

Gropper & Sons (a jobber company) and Peltier Glass Company which read as follows:

"Whereas the parties hereto desire to make an arrangement under which Peltier Co. is to manufacture marbles and Gropper Co. is to sell same and the parties are to divide the profits in the manner hereinafter set forth:

NOW, in order to set forth the various provisions of this agreement and in consideration of the mutual agreements herein set forth, IT IS AGREED between the parties as follows:

FIRST: Four machines for the manufacture of marbles shall be purchased immediately by Gropper Co. and Peltier Co. - -the cost thereof to be borne, two-thirds by Gropper Co. and one third by Peltier Co. – and title to said machines shall remain in the aforesaid parties in that proportion. The style of machine shall be approved by both parties before purchase.

Peltier Co. agrees to extend its factory so as to provide for the proper manufacture of marbles with said machines and will supply all other equipment and material that may be necessary for the operation of said machines – the cost of said equipment and materials, to be borne by the Peltier Co. and said equipment and materials to remain their property. Peltier Co. agrees to so arrange its plant as to provide for the most advantageous and economical operation of said machines.

SECOND: Gropper Co. will use its best efforts to sell the marbles manufactured by Peltier Co. Peltier Co. agree to manufacture the marbles in a first class manner, equal in quality to those of other high class manufacturers of similar merchandise and the same to be manufactured to the reasonable satisfaction of Gropper Co.

THIRD: The Peltier Co. agree promptly to install the machines purchased in their plant and to manufacture marbles – granting to Gropper Co. full opportunity to observe the manufacture. If within four months after the machines are installed Peltier Co. has not produced marbles in quantity, reasonable satisfactory to Gropper Co., then Gropper Co. shall have the right to terminate this contract without liability on the part of either to the other, and in that event Gropper Co. shall be entitled to take possession of the machines for the purpose of placing them with another manufacturer, Gropper Co. will reimburse Peltier Co. for their investment in the machines and title thereto shall then vest entirely in Gropper Co.

FOURTH: Should Peltier Co. succeed in manufacturing satisfactory marbles in quantity, then the plan of merchandising between the parties shall be as follows: Peltier Co. will manufacture marbles, pack same in containers in anticipation of shipment on orders to be received, and will hold said marbles at its *place of business subject to such orders. Peltier Co. will keep Gropper Co. advised weekly of the amount of marbles manufactured, the amount shipped and the amount on hand".*

This is only a portion of the original contract that we believe important and beneficial to marble collectors. At this time, the Peltier Company had no idea of how to make marbles and so hired Arnold Fiedler on September 15, 1924. He was recommended by Gropper to be marble maker, foreman, teacher and glass chemist. Fiedler began working that October for a contracted two year period at $100 a week, but was soon let go because he failed to produce profitability for the company. Sellers Peltier took over all of Fiedler's duties on a full-time basis. It appears Fiedler was with Peltier less than a year.

AKRO AGATE VS PELTIER GLASS COMPANY PATENT SUIT

Between 1929 and 1932 the Akro Agate Company, in a very aggressive attempt to maintain its monopoly in the machine-made marble industry, brought on two marble machine patent infringement suits against those whom they felt had wronged the Akron giant. The first, against Peltier Glass, and that company's use of the Miller machine and second, against Master Marble for use of its machine designed by John F. Early, who had previously been employed by Akro Agate to improve and design machines for that company Akro Agate contended that both Peltier and Master had infringed on patents previously issued to Akro.

It is interesting to consider, as an historical footnote, that the Akro Company, in an attempt to obtain information concerning the goings-on at Master Marble, sent an Akro employee to covertly examine the Master Marble premises. He was caught on Master property, arrested, and convicted of trespassing. The Akro Agate Company paid the fine to have their industrial spy released from jail. It is not known if Akro Agate attempted any such action at Peltier Glass. Akro at least had copies of the Peltier and Master blue prints and machine specifics easily obtained from the U.S. Patent Office.

The case against Peltier Glass was brought to the United States District Court for the Northern District of Illinois Eastern Division. The Peltier Glass Company, in case 5225, was the defendant in the 1929 lawsuit by which the Akro Agate Company charged that Peltier's marble-making machine

2-THE PELTIER GLASS COMPANY HISTORY

(William J. Miller's 1926 patent 1,601,699) was an infringement of the Horace C. Hill 1915 machine, patent 1,164,718.

The attorneys for Akro were armed with abundant testimony and diagrams with which they contended showed a marked similarity between the two company's machines.

A Mr. Wadsworth testified that made it appear that the only difference the plaintiff's and defendant's machines is that in the plaintiff's machine the rolls were of different diameters and thus rotated at different peripheral speeds; while in the defendant's machine the diameters and peripheral speeds were the same. Mr. Wadworth concluded with testimony of a technical nature indicating that the plane of the axes of the rolls relative to the horizon varies in different machines but, importantly, that the average inclination of the two axes with respect to the horizontal is around 40 degrees. Thus the later machine (Peltier) resembled too closely that of the Akro machine. Akro should therefore win its claim. The result of the rather lengthy trial was that the court ruled in favor of the Akro Agate Company, plaintiff in this case.

Naturally, the ruling was appealed by Peltier Glass. The case was heard in the United States Circuit Court of Appeals for the Seventh District, case number 4089.

In their concluding comments, after all the evidence had been rehashed before the Appeals Court, the attorneys for the Akro Agate Company summed up the whole affair in one nice and tidy package, stating: "The whole course of the defendant's manufacture has been a brazen attempt to pirate the plaintiff's business by the appropriation of the invention of the patent in suit. The plaintiff's business has been long established; since 1914 it has sold more than 667 million marbles; and up to the time of the defendant's infringement the public and this defendant had acquiesced in the validity of the patent in suit. The defendant has been free to manufacture marbles on machines similar to that formerly used by the (MF) Christensen Company of Akro, Ohio, but, instead, it has chosen because of the superior character and product of the patented machine to appropriate the plaintiff's invention.

In deciding the question here involved it is proper for the court to consider the commercial situation in giving proper weight to the patent in suit.

We submit that the patent in suit is valid, that neither the art nor the Patent Office proceedings limit it, that the defendant's machine infringes because it comes within the range of equivalents to which the patent in

2-THE PELTIER GLASS COMPANY HISTORY

suit is entitled, and that the plaintiff is entitled to an injunction and an accounting with costs. A decree in accordance with the prayer of the bill is accordingly requested".

By the time the dust had settled by mid 1930's, the original suit by the Akro Agate Company had been overturned in the Appeals Court in favor of Peltier Glass. Meanwhile, Master Marble had won all of its suits with Akro. To complicate matters still, by mid 1930's, a whole new crop of companies had been in and out of the business of producing toy glass marbles or still in the business. Foremost among these new companies were Christensen Agate Company, Vitro Agate Company, Ravenswood Novelty Works and Alley Agate Company.

In a 1980's interview with author/historian Dennis Webb, the late Roger Howdyshell of Marble King, stated that; "The breaking of the patent was the most significant event in the history of the U.S. Marble Industry".

PELTIER AND MARBLE KING

In 1949 the marble company of Lawrence E. Alley of St. Marys, West Virginia, was sold due to failing health of the owner. On June 1, 1949, the deed to the marble factory in St. Marys was transferred to Berry Pink, the well known "Marble King". On November 30, 1949 it was recorded in the office of the County Clerk of Pleasants County, West Virginia that a new marble company was starting business to be known as Marble King. Recorded shares were as follows: Barry Pink 49 shares, Lucius Coleman 1 share and Adele Rubin 1 share. All addresses are listed as the Empire State Building, 5th Avenue, New York. This accounts for 51 percent of the shares.

The authors of American Machine-Made Marbles have been told repeatedly by many sources, including the late Dennis Webb, who interviewed Roger Howdyshell of Marble King, that the fourth owner, that is, the owner of 49 percent of the shares in the new company was none other than Sellers Peltier, owner of the Peltier Glass Company. Numerous attempts to positively document this claim with actual paperwork have not been successful.

It is known, however, that at various times during the early 1950'ties, Peltier marbles were sold by Marble King and Marble King marbles were packaged by Peltier. These packages do exist although not in large quantities. The authors have in their possession a quantity of Peltier packaging material recovered from several Marble King dump sites.

2-THE PELTIER GLASS COMPANY HISTORY

Peak production at Peltier were the early 1930's and the 1940's when most of the collectible and recognizable marbles were made. The company experienced the same decline in sales as did other domestic producers due to the popularity of imported cat's eye marbles in the early 1950's. Peltier did, however, enter the cat's eye market with their "Banana" style in competition with the foreign types as well as those produced domestically by Marble King, Vitro Agate, Master Glass and Heaton Agate. By the mid 1950's there was a significant drop off in the marble production domestically. Virtually all the small producers were gone as well as such large companies as Akro Agate and Ravenswood. Cheap imports of foreign made toys, the advent of television and a general change in children's choice of toys are among the many factors used to explain this decline. Peltier's total marble output for 1954 was 141 million; sales dropped by 25 percent the next year to 106 million.

If toy marbles and automotive glass remained as the bulk of Peltier output in the mid 1950's, by the 1960's it was industrial marbles and other types of glass novelties that constituted the majority of company production. The manufacture of glass tiles and candle holders were towards the top of output by volumes of sales.

The Community Business Review of April 18, 1969, states "a quite seasonal operation, 65 to 70 employees are now engaged in the present semi-automatic shop which is now headed by Duncan Peltier, third generation of his family to be engaged in the glass production business".

Duncan Peltier passed away 1973 and was succeeded by plant manager, Joseph Jankowski, who served until 1983 when he was succeeded by Karen Armstrong. Jankowski resumed the presidency in 1986. No member of the Peltier family remained in the business for some years.

Through much of the 1980's and 1990's the Peltier Glass Company made only industrial marbles, but on occasion renewed making colorful marbles as per special order. During this time of limited marble production came two of Peltier's most popular newer marbles; "Rootbeer Float" and the "Nova".

2-THE PELTIER GLASS COMPANY HISTORY

Above left: An example of "Rootbeer Float", a white thick ribbon is floating in transparent amber base glass. Above right: This is an example of "Nova". There were different color combinations of "Nova" produced, but this color combination is more well known by collectors. Couple of orange ribbons on a jet black base glass.

These two marbles were made at the same time, October 27, 1988 by George Zellers, who ran the furnace feed and Jerry Eich, who ran the machines. George Zellers actually named the "Rootbeer Float". Both marbles are typically around 7/8" in size and were made for a marble collector from California.

 In 2002 marble history researcher David Tamulevich reported that Boyce Lundstrum, one of the three new owners of Peltier Glass, who purchased the company in November, 2001, had huge plans for the company and to turn the Peltier Mansion into a museum.

By the time Tamulevich had interviewed Lundstrum, the latter had already made two experimental marble runs; One in January, 2002, consisting of white and blue marbles in a clear base glass and were called "First Run". The "Second Run" was made in May, 2002 and the marbles contain a more varied combination of colors. The amount of marbles in this latter run equals about 4 five gallon buckets. The authors are noting that these two short production of marbles were not produced in Peltier factory and are not of the actual history of Peltier Glass marbles, but only a footnote for future generations.

After the Akro Agate Company lost the marble machine patent suits to Peltier Glass and Master Marble, there followed a flood of toy glass production by numerous companies both big and small in the era known

2-THE PELTIER GLASS COMPANY HISTORY

as "The Breaking of the Patent". Most marble collectors and dealers agree that no company, with the possible exception of the Akro Agate Company, produced as great variety of marble styles and colors than did Peltier Glass. It may be asserted too, that Peltier marbles are more easily recognizable than those of any other company.

It has been well documented elsewhere, notably in the book American Machine-Made Marbles, that while all of the major toy glass marble makers of the 1930's made the beautiful toy marbles that are so very much valued and collected today, the bread and butter for these companies was the production of industrial and the so-called game marbles; the one color opaques commonly used in such games as Chinese Checkers and Aggravation. While these latter marbles have little value to collectors unless in original packaging, they are still around and those games are still played nearly 80 years later. In fact, Chinese checker craze that swept the country in the 1930's was felt at Peltier Glass to the tune of 3.5 million of this type marbles being shipped from the plant each day. This was the equivalent of about one boxcar load.

In recent years there have been numerous documentaries on "how marbles are made" and several television shows have aired showcasing marble production at both Marble King and JABO Inc. The Akro Agate Company was highlighted in a West Virginia industry documentary in 1946. The Peltier Glass Company had them all beat. An article in The Daily Republican Of October 3, 1939, by Win Gree, reported that Paramount Pictures movie producer Ray Fernstrom was in Ottawa along with "Marble King" Berry Pink to make a color movie about the making of marbles. This film was part of the movie company's "Here's How" series shown in theaters.

The article by Green begins with this statement: "Three million marbles are rolling into existence daily at the marvelous Peltier Glass Works in north Ottawa to help supply a demand for the game which cave men started with pebbles".

The article continues: "Sellers Peltier, president and general manager, has long shunned attention for this plant but approved Paramount's dramatizing the work done there as an aid to the sale of marbles, which of course, means more employment for the factory".

The article goes on to say that marble machines like those at Peltier can't be bought. Mr. Peltier may be seen studying new possibilities of improving equipment that to the outsider appears to be working perfectly. He'll confer at length with the machine's attendant. His men are encouraged to think about improvements. There's a notice on the wall that states that new patents are wanted. It is signed "S.H.P.".

PELTIER AND KOKOMO GLASS

In 1939, Peltier Glass Company conducted some business with another glass works that produced the same type of output as did Peltier. This firm was the Kokomo Opalescent Glass Company of Kokomo, Indiana. It is interesting that these two companies used the same fine quartz sand from the same sand pits in Ottawa, Illinois.

A printed fact sheet distributed by Kokomo Opalescent Glass Company states; "From 1939 until 1942 we manufactured marbles on a machine we purchased from Peltier Glass of Ottawa, Illinois. Never realizing a satisfactory profit from the marble operation, we sold the machine back to Peltier in 1942". An addendum says; "1943, 1944, 1945".

Another short note about Peltier Glass Company marbles is necessary at this time. Marble sizes were first standardized by the M.F. Christensen Company in the first decade of the 20th Century and were subsequently followed by most makers including Peltier. Sizes were as follows: No. 000 – ½", No. 00 – 9/16", No. 0 – 5/8", No. 1 – 11/16", No. 2 – ¾", No. 3 – 13/16", No. 4 – 7/8", No. 5 – 15/16", No. 6 – 1".

Peltier Glass Company had for their Pee Wee marble size 3/8". Peltier Glass used these marbles to make very attractive necklaces which these days may be occasionally found in antique and collectable shops.

EARLY PRODUCTION

Above: An early production box of "Cerise Agates" from Peltier. The box seems to be in excellent condition. Marty Ruhland collection.

The first production of Peltier marble inventory was completed in June of 1925. Marbles produced at this time were:

Cerise Agates Marbles Marbles Produced		Agate Marbles Marbles Produced		Onyx Marbles Marbles Produced	
No.00	6,295	No.00	396,372	No.00	79,606
No.0	235,628			No.0	1,945,250
No.1	224,037			No.1	2,113,290
No.2	100,723			No.2	1,058,894
No.3	26,849			No.3	245,445
		Grand Total 6,432,349			

3-EARLY PRODUCTION

Above: An original early production box of "National Milkies" in excellent condition. Marbles look to be similar to other companies "Moonies". Gropper was an early distributor of Peltier marbles. They had exclusive rights to sell Peltier marbles from about 1924 to 1931. Marty Ruhland collection.

    Peltier commented that the smaller sizes were more difficult to produce than the larger sizes. At this time, Peltier wrote to Gropper & Son and said: "We now feel that we have passed the pioneering stage and from now on will have started to make marbles on a profitable basis. The period we have passed through was more or less purely development". By June 30, 1926, 3 groups of marbles were still being made.

3-EARLY PRODUCTION

Above: A very rare "Opal Agates" box with some green tinted marbles. The marbles seem to be opalescent. Hansel De Souza collection.

Marbles and colors were Onyx; green, royal blue, amber, white, purple & azure blue. In this inventory colors never mentioned were "Cerise Agates" and "Prima Agates". The 1926 American Wholesale Corporation, Baltimore stimulators catalog described Cerise Glass Marbles as Red Agates and Prima Cornelian as a beautiful combination of mottled colors, dark and light gray with red predominating, inventory dated June 30, 1926.

Above: A superb example of early "National Milkies" box with complete set of marbles. Hansel DeSouza collection.

25

3-EARLY PRODUCTION

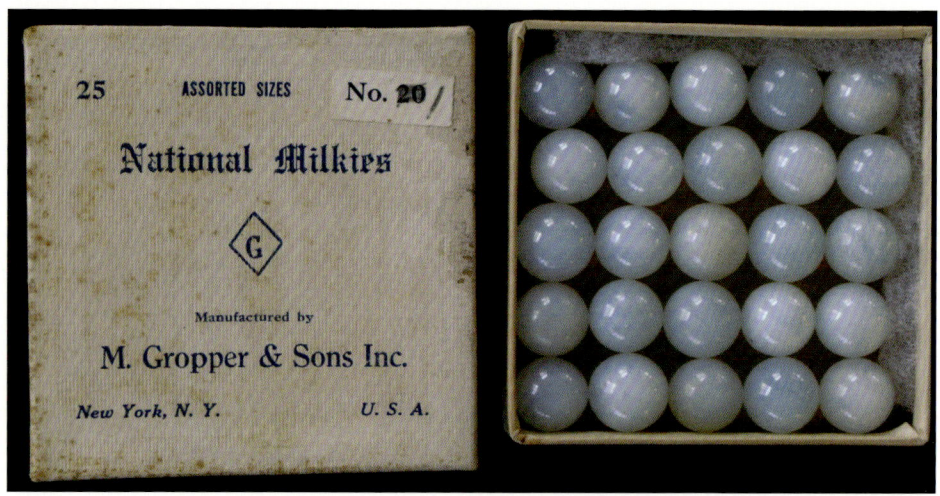

Above: Another complete set of "National Milkies" box. Number 1 indicates that the marbles are 11/16" in diameter. Hansel DeSouza collection.

There are three boxes that contain Prima Agates; 1st is orange flat box, 25, No. 0 National Prima M. Gropper and Sons. 2nd is sample kit box, National Onyx marbles, M. Gropper & Sons. 3rd is an orange flat 100 count box, national Onyx Toy Marbles No. 0, M. Gropper and Sons.

Above: A perfect example of National Prima box. Some bits and pieces sprinkled around to box to show different examples found in the Peltier site. Marbles resemble Christensen Agate American Agates". Marty Ruhland collection.

3-EARLY PRODUCTION

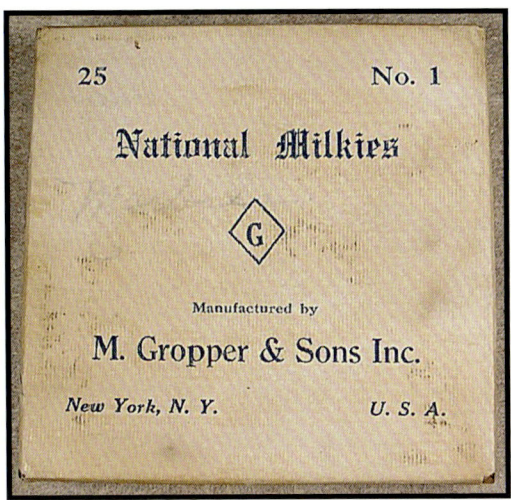

Above: A close up view of "National Milkies" early production Peltier Glass box. No 1 indicates the marbles are 11/16" in diameter. It is a 25 count box. The box seems to be in excellent condition. Gropper & Sons are claiming they are the manufacturers. Charles Williams collection.

Above: A close up view of "National Prima" early production Peltier Glass box. No 0 indicates the marbles are 5/8" in diameter. It is a 25 count box. The box seems to be in excellent condition. Gropper & Sons are claiming they are the manufacturers. Charles Williams collection.

27

4- MILLER SWIRLS

MILLER SWIRLS

Above: A magnificent example of early Miller swirl. This is called a "Tiger". Black aventurine ribbons on bright orange base glass. Peltier continued producing this color marbles until end of 1930's and the "Tiger" was one of the favorite color combinations of the children. 11/16" in diameter.

At the Peltier Glass Company marble production began with the first contract between Gropper and Peltier Glass on August 18, 1924. The first marble inventory at Peltier was made in June of 1925. It is very possible that the original decision to start marble production may have been made in response to one of two things; namely to fulfill a need to find a use for left over scrap glass from their other production items (The Kokomo

4- MILLER SWIRLS

Opalescent Glass Company did the same thing a few years later), but, secondly and perhaps more interestingly Peltier must have been aware of the tremendous success of the Akro Agate.

Above: This is a Miller swirl "Rebel" with red and black ribbons swirling on a white base glass. This example has a ying yang pattern in addition to multilayered Miller pattern. Cutlines are not too visible like National Line Rainbos. Although smaller Miller swirls are known, these types typically are found in larger sizes. This one is larger than usual at 27/32" in diameter.

Company of Clarksburg, West Virginia. Akro Agate was the giant of the industry and at that time had no real competition.

Thus we have William J. Miller entering the picture. Miller constructed a marble machine as early as 1925 (according to later court documents) that was patented in 1926 with patent number 1,601, 699. This was the first machine to be used by the Peltier Glass Company. Later on other machines were built and patented by Sellers Peltier and others.

4- MILLER SWIRLS

Much has been said and written about the Miller machine and marbles made on it. However, it must be noted that this machine is different from the machines used in the industry today. The machine built by Miller was only semi-automatic and in fact was used only to make the marbles round as it consisted of mainly two heliocentric rollers with a gravity flow, which rounded the marbles into their finished form. How the glass was arranged in the tank and the glass flow from the tank to the feeder gave the marbles their distinctive and recognizable appearance.

Today collectors call early Peltier swirls as "Miller Swirls" that are rare, have multi-ribbon configuration with a single cutline sometimes mixing with the pattern. Regardless if these marbles were made in early years or Miller machine had anything to do with it, this type of marbles deserve a chapter on their own.

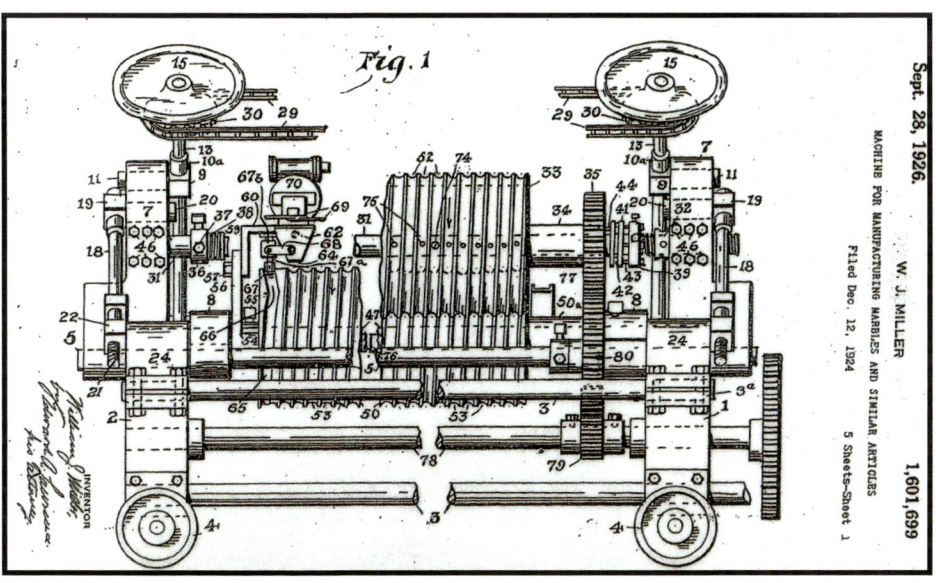

Above is the original patent drawing of the Miller machine. This machine is responsible for rounding the marble and not for the actual pattern. Obviously something must have changed and these marbles were not continued to be produced as they are not easy to find. Per minute production, rejection rate and glass compatibility were prime reasons for the machines were improved to survive in a competitive market. National Line Rainbo swirls came after the early production and lasted about a decade when later Rainbos were introduced with standard 5/8" size, simpler pattern, ribbons not as deep as NLR swirls and more on the surface, more bleeding of the colors etc.

31

4- MILLER SWIRLS

Above right: This exceptionally rare marble has grey mixed with green ribbons in addition to red ribbons on white base glass. Not a typical "Grey Coat" since there is green in the ribbons. I am calling it a "Green Coat". This marble is ¾" in diameter. Bill Tite collection.
Above left: This is a superb example of Peltier Glass "Ketchup & Mustard". The pattern represents what collectors refer today as early Miller swirls. This marble is ¾" in size. Bill Bass collection.

Above right: A rare early Peltier Miller swirl that is called "Blue Zebra". This marble has blue ribbons on white base glass. Later NLR examples showed blue aventurine but early Miller swirls mostly did not have aventurine. 13/16" in diameter. Bill Tite collection.
Above left: A blended Ketchup & Mustard in Miller pattern. Yellow ribbons are sitting on top of red ribbons just like a "Burnt Christmas Tree" or a "Burnt Rebel". So we can call this one a "Burnt K&M". 23/32" in diameter. Bill Bass collection.

4- MILLER SWIRLS

Above right: A super busy Miller "Spiderman" swirl. ¾" in diameter. Chad Kline collection.
Above left: This example is called a "Superboy". The ribbons are orange instead of red over turquoise base glass. 23/32" in diameter. Chad Kline collection.

Above right: A Miller "Orange Zebra". Fantastic pattern with busy orange ribbons on white base glass. 11/16" in diameter. Kevin Plummer collection.
Above left: A "Red Zebra" with rich red ribbons swirling wildly on white base glass. 23/32" in diameter. Kevin Plummer collection.

4- MILLER SWIRLS

Above right: A magnificent example of early Miller "Rebel" swirl. Hard to tell if there is aventurine but the pattern is very desirable. ¾" diameter. Bill Bass collection.
Above left: A rare marble as is and it is a Miller swirl. This is a "Grey Coat". Grey ribbons lay on top of red ribbons with a fantastic pattern. 25/32" in diameter. Bill Bass collection.

Above right: A classic color combination with a superb pattern. This is a Miller "Superman" swirl. Red and yellow ribbons swirling on a turquoise base glass. ¾" in diameter. Bill Tite collection.
Above left: A ying yang pattern with Miller configuration makes this marble special. The red ribbons are a little burnt, but it is still a Miller "Christmas Tree". 11/16" in diameter.

4- MILLER SWIRLS

Above right: A super rare color combination and add to that the fact it has Miller pattern. This is a "Blue Panther". Black ribbons on rich powder blue base glass. ¾" in diameter.
Above left: Another picture of the previous marble. A Miller "Blue Panther". The black ribbons typically contain very little or no aventurine on "Blue Panthers". ¾" in diameter. Kevin Plummer collection.

Above left & right: Two shots of the same marble. This is a Miler "Zebra" swirl. Black ribbons, which most of the time contain black aventurine, on white base glass. Beautiful pattern all around, which most collectors look for. Marble is ¾" in diameter. Kevin Plummer collection.

35

4- MILLER SWIRLS

Above left & right: Two shots of the same marble. This is an absolutely gorgeous Miller "Spiderman" swirl. Red ribbons swirling wildly on a turquoise base glass. The pattern is balanced all the way around. 13/16" in diameter. Kevin Plummer collection.

Above right: A special and very rare marble. This is a Miller "Bumble Bee". Black ribbons on yellow base glass. This example is not only a rare Miller swirl, but also contains green aventurine on the ribbons. 23/32" in diameter. Clyde Tuller collection. Above left: An incredible pattern on this Miller "Christmas Tree". Red ribbons look to be a little burnt. 5/8" in diameter. Mark and Dana Forrester collection.

4- MILLER SWIRLS

Above left & right: Black ribbons loaded with aventurine swirling wildly on brilliant red base glass. This is a rare example of Miller swirl "Wasp". Marble is 21/32" in diameter. Clyde Tuller collection.

Above right: A Miller "Christmas Tree". The pattern is outstanding on this example. ¾" in diameter.
Above left: Almost the same marble. Size, colors and pattern are very similar.

37

4- MILLER SWIRLS

Above right: A Miller "Rebel" swirl. The red ribbons are nice dark and the black ribbons contain aventurine. The marble is in ¾" in diameter.
Above left: This is a shooter Miller "Superman" marble. This classic color combination consists of red and yellow ribbons on a turquoise base glass. ¾" in diameter.

Above right: This unusual example is an "Orange Christmas Tree". The ribbons are orange instead of red with forest green ribbons. ¾" in diameter.
Above left: A shooter Miller "Christmas Tree". Forest green and red ribbons on white base. ¾" in diameter.

4- MILLER SWIRLS

Above right: A magnificent "Zebra" swirl. Thick black ribbons are absolutely loaded with aventurine. Note that there is more than typical 4 ribbons on this example. 23/32" in diameter.
Above left: A Miller "Rebel" swirl. The ribbons are thinner and a wonderful pattern all around. ¾" in diameter.

Above right & left: Two shots of the same marble. This is a Submarine "Cubscout". Yellow ribbons swirling on a translucent or transparent blue base glass. A spectacular pattern all around. Marble is a desirable ¾" in diameter.

4- MILLER SWIRLS

Above right: A gorgeous pattern on this National Line Rainbo "Spiderman" swirl. Bright red ribbons swirling in a wonderful pattern on turquoise base glass. 21/32" in diameter.

Above left: A very hard to find marble. This is a "Burnt Rebel". Black ribbons sitting on top of burnt red ribbons. This example has aventurine in the black ribbons which is even harder to find. 23/32" in diameter.

Above right: This marble could easily be in the "Rarities" chapter. A rare "Blue Wasp". Blue ribbons loaded with saphire blue aventurine on red base glass. 11/16" in diameter.

Above left: Another rarity is this Miller "Tiger" swirl. Thin black ribbons, loaded with black aventurine, on a brilliant orange base glass. 23/32" in diameter.

4- MILLER SWIRLS

Above right: White ribbons swirling wildly on a transparent red base glass. A spectacular pattern. Could it be an early Miller swirl? 11/16" in diameter. Bill Bass collection.
Above left: Wonderful Miller pattern with blending colors on this "Superman". Charles Williams collection.

Above right: Thin brownish red ribbons swirling on a white base glass. A huge example in 7/8" in diameter. Bill Bass collection.
Above left: A super busy pattern on this Miller "Christmas Tree" swirl. Kevin Plummer collection.

4- MILLER SWIRLS

Above right and left: Two shots of the same marble. The pattern just doesn't get any better than this transparent red based swirl marble. Multiple white ribbons swirling all around. It could definitely be a Miller swirl. Charles Williams collection.

Above right: Thin blue ribbons swirling on white base glass. This is a "Blue Zebra". A hard to find marble. This marble is ¾" in diameter. Bill Bass collection.

Above left: A magnificent example of a Miller "Superboy" swirl. Red with yellow and orange highlights on a turquoise base glass. This is a large shooter size marble at 7/8" in diameter. Bill Bass collection.

42

4- MILLER SWIRLS

Above right: Yellow ribbons blended with orange red ribbons on a white base glass. This is a blended Ketchup & Mustard swirl. 11/16" in diameter.
Above left: Black ribbons loaded with silver aventurine swirling wildly on a gorgeous red base glass. This is a "Wasp" with Miller pattern. The marble is 11/16" in diameter.

Above right: Emerald green ribbons swirling in a balanced way all around on a golden yellow base glass. This marble is a "John Deer" swirl. 23/32" in diameter.
Above left: Bright yellow ribbons on turquoise base glass. This is a "Cubscout" swirl. 11/16" in diameter.

43

4- MILLER SWIRLS

Above right: This unusual hybrid "Christmas Tree" marble is showing a mint green ribbons with brownish red ribbons on white base glass. ¾" in diameter. Kevin Plummer collection.
Above left: This huge shooter "Golden Rebel is in 7/8" in diameter. They don't get much larger than this and a great pattern too. Bill Bass collection.

Above right & left: Two shots of the same marble. A "Burnt Christmas Tree" with a swirl pattern. Hard to tell how early these types of marbles are in Peltier production but probably earlier than later. This type of marble has green ribbons sitting on top of burnt brown ribbons. This example is 23/32" in diameter.

44

4- MILLER SWIRLS

Above right: Another view of the Miller Superman that is on the cover. It is an extraordinary example with a superb pattern. ¾" in size. Jeff Wichmann collection.
Above left: This Golden Rebel is shown in this book in different pages. Here is another great shot. 13/16" in size.
Above left: This is a Miller "Burnt Rebel". Black ribbons sitting on top of red ribbons swirling wildly on a white base glass. There is light amount of aventurine in the black. 23/32" in size.

45

THREE COLOR NATIONAL LINE RAINBOS

Above: A magnificent example of "Golden Rebel". This 3 color National Line Rainbo marble has thick black ribbons absolutely loaded with black aventurine. Also the rich red ribbons add additional eye appeal on a bright golden yellow base glass.

National Line Rainbos are arguably the most looked after collectible antique machine made marbles. Peltier Glass Company started producing them in late 1920's and continued until late 1930's. Later production went on to Rainbos until the end of marble production. Collectors affectionately named these colorful marbles and these names for some reason sticked to them. In this chapter we are going to concentrate on the three color NLRs. Peltier produced and sticked to the same color combinations throughout the years. Some color combinations were produced less and are rarer then the others. It is still a mystery why some of the most beautiful color combinations were not produced more in numbers. Glass compatibility and rejection might be one of the reasons that we can consider.

5 - THREE COLOR NATIONAL LINE RAINBOS

Above right: An "Orange Rebel" with a nice loop design. This is a very popular pattern by collectors and orange ribbons are rarer than the typical red ribbons. 11/16" in size. Bill Bass collection.
Above left: A "Golden Rebel". Four red and two black aventurine ribbons on a yellow base glass. Cutlines close to each other. 21/32" size. Bill Bass collection.

Above right: This is a "Christmas Tree". Bright green and red ribbons on a white base glass. This example has an interesting pattern with some blending showing. 23/32" size. Bill Bass collection.
Above left: Every collectors dream: A "Blue Galaxy". Although the yellow ribbons are not that bright in this example, collectors value this marble very highly. 5/8" in diameter. Bill Bass collection.

5 - THREE COLOR NATIONAL LINE RAINBOS

Above right: Blue and red ribbons on a white base glass will give you a "Liberty". Red ribbons are wide and thinned down a bit. Bill Bass collection.
Above left: This is a "Ketchup & Mustard". What is special about this example is the yellow ribbons sit on top of red ribbons, which technically makes this a "Burnt Ketchup & Mustard".

Above right: A "Liberty" with a magnificent pattern. Ribbons are not wide and evenly spaced on white base glass.
Above left: This marble could easily qualify for the rarities chapter. This is a "Christmas Tree" with aventurine. The dark forest green ribbons are loaded with green aventurine. Red ribbons are typically transparent on these type of Christmas Trees. These are very rare and highly desirable. Kevin Plummer collection.

5 - THREE COLOR NATIONAL LINE RAINBOS

Above right and left: Two shots of the same marble. This extraordinary example of "Golden Rebel" has two cutlines close to each other and a loop at the other end. Black ribbons are loaded with aventurine. 13/16" in diameter. Kevin Plummer collection.

Above right and left: This is another double shot of another museum piece. This "Golden Rebel" has a wonderful loop at one end and the other end shows wide black ribbons absolutely loaded with aventurine. Shooter "Golden Rebels" are highly desirable for collectors. 13/16" in diameter. Kevin Plummer collection.

5 - THREE COLOR NATIONAL LINE RAINBOS

Above right and left: Here is one more double shot of an unusual and a rare example of "Golden Rebel". What is so interesting on this example is one pole is showing a "9" pattern, which is typically seen on earlier handgathered, machine rounded marbles. This one may not be handgathered but still a super rare example. Mark and Dana Forrester collection.

Above right: A "Golden Rebel" with flashy aventurine. Peltier produced Golden Rebels in almost all sizes, but interestingly they are found more in larger sizes. Maybe a special run. Clyde Tuller collection.
Above left: Red and yellow ribbons on turquoise base glass. This is a classic "Superman". This example is showing no blends, which is sometimes a desired effect. Chad Kline collection.

51

5 - THREE COLOR NATIONAL LINE RAINBOS

Above right and left: Two shots of the same "Superman". This example has darker yellow ribbons and cutlines that are close to each other. The blending colors give an extra eye appeal to this type of Superman. Magnificent specimen with a superb pattern. 11/16" in diameter. Dani and Ernie Kirk collection.

Above right: This large example of "Superman" showing a nice yellow ribbon and couple red ribbons. Large Supermans are very hard to find in good condition such as this example. 25/32" in diameter.
Above left: This "Ketchup and Mustard" is showing a beautiful pattern with some blends. Ribbon thickness is well balanced. A very desirable example. ¾" in diameter.

52

5 - THREE COLOR NATIONAL LINE RAINBOS

Above right & left: This is a two shot of the same marble. Green ribbons sit on top of burnt brown ribbons. This marble is named appropriately "Burnt Christmas Tree". Most of these types are found swirly with cutlines hard to define, but this example has three definite cutlines. Two of them close to each other and another one on the other side. A National Line Rainbo era marble. ¾" in diameter.

Above right: A superb example of another "Superman". Four red ribbons and two yellow ribbons on a turquoise base glass. Yellow ribbons thin down and blend a little to show some green blends. 21/32" in diameter.
Above left: A "Christmas Tree" with a nice loop pattern. The base glass has a cream tone and a great condition. 11/16" in diameter.

53

5 - THREE COLOR NATIONAL LINE RAINBOS

Above right: A "Christmas Tree" with a wonderful loop pattern. This marble almost gives an early handgathered feeling. It is a swirly National Line Rainbo. 21/32" in diameter.
Above left: Another "Christmas Tree" with a lot of red showing. The red ribbons are transparent and there are some blends in the green. 11/16" in diameter.

Above right: A beautiful "Liberty" with blue and red ribbons on white base glass. The pattern almost looks like an American flag. 11/16" in diameter.
Above left: A "Rebel" with cutlines very close to each other. A very desirable and overall balanced pattern. 11/16" in diameter.

5 - THREE COLOR NATIONAL LINE RAINBOS

Above right: This is an "Orange Rebel" with burnt orange ribbons replacing typical red ribbons. The ribbons are nice and thick which gives an extra interest to the marble. 11/16" in diameter.
Above left: A "Superman" with some blending. This example has a nice swirly pattern and with the blends it is very desirable to collectors. 21/32" in diameter.

Above right: This superb example of "Christmas Tree" has thinner ribbons but they are overall very well balaced and magnificent pattern. The marble almost could be qualified as an early Miller swirl, but the autor believes it is still a NLR. 11/16" in diameter.
Above left: Another gorgeous "Christmas Tree" with bold straight ribbon configuration. Interesting to note that there are three red and three green ribbons instead of 4 to 2 configuration.

5 - THREE COLOR NATIONAL LINE RAINBOS

Above right: This is a hard to find "Burnt Ketchup & Mustard" where the yellow ribbons sit on top of red ribbons. Red ribbons do not show much brown like "Burnt Rebels" or Burnt Christmas Trees", but it is still technically the same type. 23/32" in diameter.
Above left: This "Rebel" is showing a fantastic swirly pattern with an overall balanced ribbon configuration. 11/16" in diameter.

Above right: This "Liberty" has a thick and deep blue ribbons creating a loop on one pole. Great eye appeal. 11/16" in diameter.
Above left: This "Burnt Christmas Tree" could be classified as a Miller swirl, but with the cutlines showing clearly I chose to place it in this chapter. These examples are typically very swirly and larger than typical sizes. 23/32" in diameter.

5 - THREE COLOR NATIONAL LINE RAINBOS

Above right: This magnificent marble is borderline a "Burnt Chritmas Tree, but the red ribbons are separate. Green ribbons are definitely a little burnt and the base color is deep cream. A gorgeous pattern also.
Above left: A very hard to find "Burnt Rebel". This superb example is showing black ribbons that are loaded with aventurine, sitting on top of red ribbons. Cutlines are close to each other. A great example.

Above right: This "Superman" has straight ribbons with no blending. Strong colors and simple, classic pattern makes it a special example.
Above left: A magnificent "Christmas Tree" with a pattern that would fit in any Art Deco description. These marbles were made during Art Deco period and with a little imagination the connection can be established.

5 - THREE COLOR NATIONAL LINE RAINBOS

Above right and left: Two shots of the same marble. This is the elusive "Blue Galaxy". For some reason Peltier did not produce many of these and one theory for that is the glass compatibility. There are a lot of examples with air pops and other as made imperfections that may have limited larger type examples. Yellow and black aventurine ribbons on turquoise base glass. The swirling and pattern on this example is one of the better ones we have seen. 21/32" in diameter.

Above right: The base color of this "Superman" is as good as it gets. A rich, dark turquoise color. Ribbons do not show any blending and a great size too. 11/16".
Above left: A swirly "Golden Rebel". The pattern shows few cutlines and foldlines with thinner ribbons swirling on a golden yellow base glass. Black ribbons are loaded with aventurine. 11/16" in diameter.

5 -THREE COLOR NATIONAL LINE RAINBOS

Above right and left: Two shots of the same marble. This is a rare "Orange Rebel". Orange ribbons and black ribbons that are loaded with aventurine on a white base glass. This example has a great pattern and a nice size too. 11/16" in diameter.

Above right: This is a "Christmas Tree" with bright colors and a nice pattern. Some blending of colors gives depth to the marble. The condition looks to be superb. 11/16" in diameter.
Above left: A "Golden Rebel" with straight ribbon configuration. 4 red ribbons and two black ribbons with aventurine on a yellow base glass. Golden Rebels almost always show black aventurine in black ribbons, which might be a proof that they are always a special run production. This one is 21/32"in diameter.

59

5 - THREE COLOR NATIONAL LINE RAINBOS

Above right: This shot and two below are the same "Golden Rebel". Wide and thick ribbons loaded with aventurine. This example is 13/16" in diameter.
Above left: A classic "Liberty" with strong coloring, fantastic pattern and superb condition. Three transparent blue ribbons and three red ribbons placed against each other on a white base glass. Hard to find ribbon configuration. 11/16" in diameter.

Above right and left: This special "Golden Rebel" showing enormous sized black ribbons that are loaded with aventurine. On top of that the red ribbons are as bright and rich as it gets. And golden yellow base glass makes this color combination a very eye appealing combo. This large example is 13/16" in diameter and high mint condition.

5 - THREE COLOR NATIONAL LINE RAINBOS

Above right and left: A very unusual example of "Rebel". This very swirly example showing a very unusual red color with black aventurine ribbons on a white base glass. This shade of red has never been seen on Peltier Glass marbles. 11/16" in diameter.

Above right: Here is a marble that deserves to be in the "Rarities" chapter. This is a "Green Rebel". Green and black aventurine ribbons on white base glass. This type always found in smaller 19/32" to 5/8" sizes except one found in ¾" in diameter that is shown in this book. Chad Kline collection.
Above left: This Peltier Glass marble is also a very rare example. Similar to the previous marble, this one is showing brown ribbons with aventurine. These marbles were produced in smaller sizes. Collectors name is "Orion's Belt". Kevin Plummer collection.

5 - THREE COLOR NATIONAL LINE RAINBOS

Above right: This marble is a "Hybrid Christmas Tree". The reason is the green ribbons are an unusual mint green and the red ribbons are brownish, almost like a burnt red. These colors are seldom found and should be a short run at the factory. 11/16"+ in diameter. Kevin Plummer collection.
Above left: This "Golden Rebel" has thin black ribbons and red ribbons on yellow. A very nice pattern on this example. Bill Bass collection.

Above right: This rare "Christmas Tree" has burnt green ribbons that are loaded with green aventurine. In addition to that the other color is orange, which is by itself a rarity. A superb pattern completes the package. 11/16" in diameter.
Above left: This is a fantastic example of "Burnt Rebel". Black aventurine ribbons sitting on top of red ribbons. The cutlines are somewhat close to each other that makes it a beautiful pattern. 23/32" in diameter.

5 - THREE COLOR NATIONAL LINE RAINBOS

Above right: This marble is a hybrid Christmas Tree/ Rebel combo. It contains green and black aventurine as well as some brown mixed in it. Bright red ribbons add a lot to the eye appeal. 21/32" in size.

Above left: This Golden Rebel is shown in this book in different pages. Here is another great shot. 13/16" in size.

Above: A fantastic collection of classic three color National Line Rainbos. Marbles look all to be from similar time runs although the Rebels might be from earlier Miller time period. The collection is put together in 2 years of collecting which proves if chased hard enough anything is possible. Marbles are all around 5/8" in size. Courtesy of Richard Tisch collection.

64

TWO COLOR NATIONAL LINE RAINBOS

Above: This marble should be directly included in the rarity chapter. It is a "Blue Panther". Black ribbons with very little amount of aventurine on rich powder blue base glass. This blue glass is different than the classic "Superman", Spiderman", Superboy", Blue Galaxy" etc. It must be a short availability or the company chose not to use this color in the long term. Whatever the reason might be, it makes this type of marble very rare and highly sought after by today's collectors. 11/16" in diameter. Sami Arim collection.

As mentioned in the previous chapter National Line Rainbos are Peltier Glass Company's golden era of marble making. It is not 100% clear when the company started making these two cutline, less swirly, strong colored marbles but it can be guessed that it started gradualy towards the end of Miller machine period. The machines were improved to produce more marbles in shorter time with less rejects and prettier patters with those day's tastes. We will cover National Line Rainbos with only two colors in this chapter.

6-TWO COLOR NATIONAL LINE RAINBOS

Above right & left: Two shots of the same marble. This is a swirly "Red Bee". This example is also showing a "ying yang" pattern that is such a big part of Peltier marbles, we decided to included a separate chapter for the pattern alone later in the book. Red ribbons thin down and blend with yellow base glass and creates a gorgeous pattern. Chuck Garrett collection.

Above right: This is a classic "Tiger". This color combination along with few others must be very popular among children at the time. Black aventurine ribbons on bright orange base glass. This example has a gorgeous pattern with flashy aventurine. Might even qualify as a Miller swirl. 23/32" in diameter.

Above left: This marble is one of the rare color combinations of the Peltier production. It should be actually in the rarity chapter. This is a "Blue Bee". Blue ribbons loaded with blue aventurine on a lemon yellow base glass. 11/16" in diameter. Bill Bass collection.

6-TWO COLOR NATIONAL LINE RAINBOS

Above right: This is a "Flaming Dragon" with aventurine. Aventurine is rarely found in "Flaming Dragons". Red with orange highlights on green base glass. Could have qualified as a three color NLR, but the lack of separate third color will prevent it. Bill Tite collection.
Above left: This is a hybrid example between a "Superboy" and a "Cubscout". All the blends give a third color appereance, but we decided to qualify it as two color NLR. Regardless, a magnificent example. Kevin Plummer collection.

Above right and left: Two shots of the same marble. We call this unusual example a "Burnt Spiderman". Ruddy red ribbons on a burnt blue base glass. We do not know what might happened for the marble come out this way but it is definitely not a run of the mill marble. 11/16" in diameter. Kevin Plummer collection.

67

6-TWO COLOR NATIONAL LINE RAINBOS

Above right and left: Two shots of the same marble. This is a "Superboy". Red ribbons with orange highlights on a turquoise base glass. This example has a fantastic pattern. There are also some blends that add eye appeal to this marble. Two cutlines are close to each other and a third cutline is on the other side of the marble. Kevin Plummer collection.

Above right and left: This is a shooter "Blue Zebra". Dark blue ribbons on a white base glass. Thick ribbons gives a very balanced pattern overall. Two cutlines are close to each other on one side. Kevin Plummer collection.

6-TWO COLOR NATIONAL LINE RAINBOS

Above right: A "Superboy" with a swirly pattern. There are some dark edges around the orange ribbons. A gorgeous example. Charles Williams collection.
Above left: Here is a "Blue Bee". The blue ribbons are loaded with blue aventurine. Ribbons meet at the cutline. The base yellow glass has always a lemonish cold hue that shows that the "Blue Bees" were a short and different run than the regular runs. Mark & Dana Forrester collection.

Above right: This is a "Red Bee". The ribbons are not as dark red as some other examples but still not orange. There are 5 ribbons that we can count which is unusual compared to typical 4 ribbon NLRs.
Above left: This is a "Ruby Bee", which is a "Red Bee" with aventurine in the red ribbons. This example also is showing a separate orange line on one red ribbon. Clyde Tuller collection.

6-TWO COLOR NATIONAL LINE RAINBOS

Above right: This is an "Orange Bee". True "Orange Bees" are not easy to find because Peltier probably used red glass for this type of marbles most of the time. This one has true orange ribbons on yellow base glass. The pattern is also gorgeous. 21/32" in diameter.

Above left: This is a "Tiger". Black aventurine ribbons on a gorgeous orange base glass. This one also has a great pattern. 11/16" in diameter.

Above right: This is a "Flaming Dragon". The orange highlights on the red ribbons are not as strong but they are there. A nice pattern, great condition and size at 11/16" in diameter.

Above left: This is a "Golden Dragon". Orange ribbons with some highlights on a custard base glass. A very nice color combination to say the least. These are not easy to find. 23/32" in diameter.

70

6-TWO COLOR NATIONAL LINE RAINBOS

Above right: This is a "John Deer". Green ribbons on a bright yellow base glass. This example is showing some darker lines at the edge of the ribbons. 21/32" in diameter.
Above left: This example is a borderline "Tiger" and a "Chocolate Cow". Still not the rare "Cow" since there is an orange and red hue at the base glass. Collectors look for a true brown for it to qualify as "Chocolate Cow". Still a very unusual and attractive base color and desirable. 43/64" in diameter.

Above right: A one of a kind "Grey Bee". Not many of these are around. Grey ribbons on yellow base glass. Could have been between the two different runs. 21/32" in diameter.
Above left: This is a "Golden Dragon". Most of the" Golden Dragons" show great classic NLR ribbon patterns. This one is no exception. Gorgeous marble. 11/16" in diameter.

6-TWO COLOR NATIONAL LINE RAINBOS

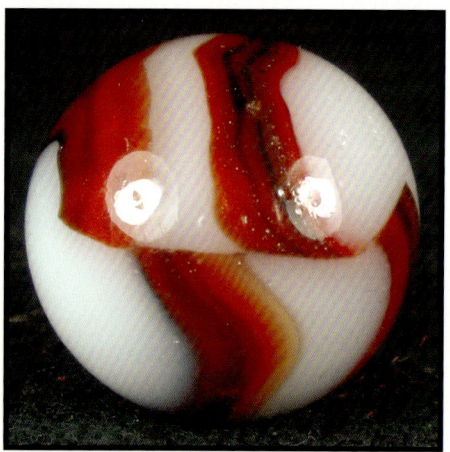

Above right: This is a "Red Bee". This example could be considered as a Miller swirl, but two cutlines and some other properties placed it to NLR category. Multiple red ribbons on yellow base glass. A superb pattern as most of this type of "Red Bees" seems to have. 11/16" in diameter.

Above left: This one should be in the aventurine chapter, but fits here too. This is a "Red Zebra" with fiery aventurine. This type of marble with aventurine is rare and highly desirable. 11/16" in diameter.

Above right: A "Tiger" with a fantastic swirl pattern. Black aventurine ribbons on orange base glass. 11/16" in diameter.

Above left: This is a "Superboy". Orange ribbons on turquoise base glass. A nice pattern with cutlines parallel to each other. 11/16" in diameter.

6-TWO COLOR NATIONAL LINE RAINBOS

Above right & left: Two shots of the same marble. The name of this marble is sometimes confused. This one is a "Lemon Lime". Dark yellow ribbons on green base glass. This example has a very attractive pattern, a balanced distribution. Not terribly rare or valuable but hard to find in nice pattern, condition and size all combined together. 11/16" in diameter.

 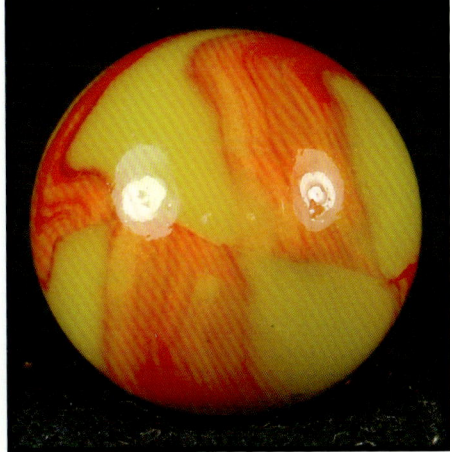

Above right: This is another "Golden Dragon". Orange ribbons on a custard yellow base glass. This example has nice and thick ribbons with perfectly offset checkerboard placement. 11/16" in diameter.
Above left: Another "Lemon Lime". Everything we said above applies to this example. Nice pattern and coloring with good 11/16" diameter size.

73

6-TWO COLOR NATIONAL LINE RAINBOS

Above right: This is a "John Deer". The name confuses with the "Lemon Lime" quite often. This type has transparent green ribbons on yellow base glass. Nice rich coloring. 11/16" in diameter.
Above left: This is a "Dragon" without the flames. Beautiful rich red ribbons swirling on a green base glass. Fantastic condition and eye appeal. 11/16" in diameter.

Above right: This example does not have a name or maybe it does, but not yet sticked to it. It is not a common marble. It may have been produced late in the NLR period. Greenish yellow ribbons on medium blue base glass. A lot of times aventurine can be found on these. 11/16" in diameter.
Above left: This is a "Wasp". Black aventurine ribbons on a rich red base glass. The ribbons boost a nice offset checkerboard pattern. 11/16" in diameter.

6-TWO COLOR NATIONAL LINE RAINBOS

Above right: This is a borderline "Golden Dragon". This example has reddish ribbons with some highlights and it just doesn't look the same. Nice offset cutline configuration. 11/16" in diameter.

Above left: A borderline "Chocolate Cow". Black aventurine ribbons on a brown base glass. Base glass is dark brown but does have a little orange and red hue. Collectors always look for true brown for their collections. 21/32" in diameter.

Above right: This is another borderline "Chocolate Cow/Wasp". Base color is a strange reddish brown. Actually really unique but still not a true "Cow", so to speak. Nice pattern. 21/32" in diameter.

Above left: This is a classic "Cubscout". Bright yellow ribbons on turquoise base glass. The "Cubscouts" are not rare but this one has nice thick ribbons, a nice size at 11/16" in diameter and a superb pattern with ribbons close to each other.

6-TWO COLOR NATIONAL LINE RAINBOS

Above right: Almost a twin to the previous example, this "Cubscout" also has a gorgeous pattern with bright yellow ribbons that are nicely balanced and have a sweet pattern. 11/16" in diameter.
Above left: This is a "Red Bee" with a remarkable pattern. Rich and dark red ribbons swirling wonderfully on a yellow base glass. Base glass showing some lighter areas which gives the marble more interest to the viewer. 11/16" in diameter.

Above right: Here is a masterful "Superboy" with a ying yang pattern. This pattern can be found in Peltier marbles quite often and is very desirable. We have a chapter covering this pattern later in the book. This example has red and orange ribbons with some yellow highlights on a turquoise base glass. 11/16" in diameter.
Above left: This is a magnificent "Wasp" with a very rich, dark red base glass. Black ribbons with aventurine over the red base show a great contrast. 11/16" in diameter.

76

6-TWO COLOR NATIONAL LINE RAINBOS

Above right: This is a "Superboy" with orange ribbons and yellow highlights and some burnt brown on a turquoise base glass. A nice pattern and superb condition. 11/16" in diameter.
Above left: This is a "Red Bee" with a wonderful checkerboard offset ribbon configuration. Colors are fantastic and a nice size at 11/16" in diameter.

Above right: This is a "John Deer" with aventurine. Green transparent ribbons are loaded with green aventurine on yellow base glass. Like any other example with aventurine this one is very hard to find and very desirable among Peltier collectors. 11/16" in diameter.
Above left: This is the elusive "Blue Zebra". This one is not only showing magnificent blue ribbons absolutely loaded with blue aventurine, but it also has an excellent pattern and nice large size at 11/16"+ in diameter. Bill Tite collection.

MULTICOLOR SWIRLS

Above: This multicolor swirl is showing an incredible pattern and coloring. Children must have fallen in love when they saw these marbles. This gorgeous marble has red, blue and white ribbons on green tinted transparent base glass. ¾" in diameter. Sami Arim collection.

Multicolor swirls often confused as Miller swirls and are thought to be produced during the same time as National Line Rainbos. They do show sometimes straight ribbon layout like any NLR but they most often then not have a swirly pattern. There are always at least 3 color plus the base glass on these marbles. Some color combinations are more common then the others. Base colors are most of the time green tinted transparent, but they could be amber or clear and even sometimes transparent blue. We will try to cover most of the color combinations in this chapter.

7-MULTICOLOR SWIRLS

Above right: This swirl actually shows one less color than the description with only red and white, but the base is green tinted transparent base and the pattern is unmistakable. ¾" in diameter.
Above left: This example is showing turquoise, orange and white on green tinted transparent base glass. 23/32" in diameter.

Above right: Probably the most common color combination. This example has turquoise, yellow and white on green tinted transparent base glass. The unusual part is there is additional oxblood on this marble. Oxblood is rarely found in multicolor swirls and is a desirable addition to any Peltier marble. 11/16" in diameter.
Abobe left: Blue, red and white ribbons on green base glass. The ribbons are very well defined and the pattern is beautiful. 23/32" in diameter.

7-MULTICOLOR SWIRLS

Above right: This Multicolor swirl has turquoise, orange and white ribbons, which is a quite common color combination. But in addition there is a nice amount of oxblood in the mix. An added bonus for the collector. 11/16" in diameter.
Above left: This example does not have three colors but still in the multicolor family. Burnt salmon and white ribbons on transparent green base glass. 11/16" in diameter.

Above right: This swirl has turquoise, red and white ribbons on transparent green base glass. The cutlines are close to each other which creates an outstanding design and pattern. 23/32" in diameter.
Above left: This color combination is not as common as the type with white ribbons instead the yellow ribbons. The colors are salmon, blue and yellow on transparent green tinted base glass. A pretty example too. 11/16" in diameter.

7-MULTICOLOR SWIRLS

Above right: Large multicolor swirls are harder to find, because probably collectors hold on to them and do not sell them often. Above two examples are some of them. Harder to find orange, green and white ribbons on transparent green tinted base glass. Not too swirly but the size makes it up. ¾" in diameter.
Above left: This magnificent swirl has only orange and white ribbons on a tinted base glass. The pattern is just out of this world and the size is huge too. ¾" in diameter.

Above right: Orange, green and white ribbons swirling wildly on a transparent tinted base glass. The pattern on this example is just fantastic. 23/32" diameter.
Above left; This swirl looks almost like a patch. Missing the white ribbon gives it a nice different eye appeal. Only green and red ribbons on a transparent amber base glass. 23/32" in diameter.

7-MULTICOLOR SWIRLS

Above right: This color combination is always harder to find in large sizes. Salmon, pale green and white ribbons on green tinted transparent base glass. This one is large in 11/16" in diameter.
Above left: A bright green, orange and white ribbons on tinted transparent base glass. A highly unusual color combination. It is a very pretty marble. 11/16" in diameter.

Above right: This example is almost an early version of later "Sunset" marbles. This one has only red and white ribbons that dive into the bubble filled clear base glass. Wonderful swirling can be viewed easily. ¾" in diameter.
Above left: This Multicolor swirl has turquoise, yellow and white, plus oxblood. A nice swirling effect makes this a great marble. 21/32" in diameter.

83

COMICS & ADVERTISING

Above: This is one of a kind 1" diameter translucent moonie base glass "Emma" comic marble. This marble does not have the second color patch all other comics typically display. This marble belongs to Larry and Kathy Runyan Swacina collection.

    One of the most collectible production marbles Peltier Glass ever produced were the "Picture Marbles", which commonly referred as "Comic" marbles. These marbles were typically on a Peerless Patch marble and were made same time as National Line Rainbos around late 1920's and late 1930'ties. The characters on the marbles were known as comics at the time period and are with the approximate increasing rarity Emma, Koko, Bimbo, Andy, Smitty, Herbie, Skeezix, Annie, Sandy, Betty, Moon and Kayo, which is considered as the rarest of the series. These characters were believed to

8-COMICS & ADVERTISING

be produced by firing black graphite at the marble and then refiring a clear glass coat on top of it. These marbles were mostly produced on a white base glass. Also yellow based comic marbles were produced in larger quatities but considered now as more valuable than white based examples. Patch colores veried greatly including red, blue, green, orange, black. Some examples with black and blue patches can be found with aventurine which adds greatly to the value. There are two additional well known character marbles Peltier Glass produced; "Tom Mix" and an advertising piece of "Coat's Master Loaf". These marbles were produced in a very limited quantity and are considered very rare. Yellow base glass color adds to the value for these two hard to find Peltier marbles. Harder to find patch colors are also an addition to rarity. Comic marbles were collectible as soon as they hit the shelves. Original packaging of these marbles have the print "Collect Them All". Since the day they were produced they are collected by children and now adult collectors of these gems.

 Below is some information which will not be supported with any additional pictures. There is a group of comic marbles found and purchased directly from the Peltier great grand daughter and were made for the family only. Reason of not including any pictures is to avoid any reproduction and forgery of these extraordinarily rare marbles and protect history.

 There are two groups of comic marbles found. Group 1 were made for and are confirmed to be the only ones made for the Peltier Family. Group 2 are very rare marbles that are not confirmed to be made for the family but are found in very limited numbers as indicated below.

 Group 1 stamped with the following on the marble: Peltier (confirmed only 3 exists), Peltier Glass Co (confirmed only 1 exists), Glass (only 1 exists), Ottawa IL (only 1 exists), Babe Ruth (One version large print only 1 exists, Babe Ruth (Small print, 1 exists), 1934 Worlds Fair (1 exists).

 Group 2 stamped with the follwing on the marble:Orange Crush (1 known exist), Coca Cola (1 known to exist), Hoover For President (3 known to exist), Worlds Fair 1933 (1 known to exist), Untied (1 known to exist), Tom Mix and Cotes Master Loaf as indicated above.

 As an addition to white and yellow based Comic marbles there were some rarer comics produced on two different shade of green and turquoise base. These colors were not produced in larger quantities most likely because darker base glass and dark print of graphite was not working well together. In this chapter harder to find green and turquoise based comics and advertising examples are shown.

8-COMICS & ADVERTISING

Above right: A "Betty" on a turquoise base glass and yellow patch. The print looks to be in great shape. 11/16" in diameter. Jamie Kummer collection.
Above left: Any comic on a turquoise base is very hard to find. This is because the images didn't show on a darker background so they didn't do many of those. This is "Koko" with a great print and red patch. 11/16" in diameter. Jamie Kummer collection.

Above right: There were two different tones of green based comic marbles produced. Both are very hard to find and were produced in limited quantities. "Emma" on the pale green base glass. The patch color is not visible on this picture. Jamie Kummer collection.
Above left: A "Kayo" on darker green base glass with yellow patch. "Kayo" is the hardest to find standart comic and this one is very rare. 11/16" in diameter. Jamie Kummer collection.

87

8-COMICS & ADVERTISING

Above right: A super rare "Kayo" on darker green base glass with yellow patch. Print seems to be in great condition. 11/16" in diameter. Jamie Kummer collection.
Above left: A "Smitty" on turquoise base glass. There is a nice large red patch in the background. The print is average, but the marble is very rare. 11/16" in diameter. Jamie Kummer collection.

Above right: A "Bimbo" on a turquoise base glass with yellow patch. Print is decent. 11/16" in diameter. Jamie Kummer collection.
Above left: "Andy" on a turquoise base glass and a large red patch. A superb print. 11/16" in diameter. Jamie Kummer collection.

8-COMICS & ADVERTISING

Above right: A thick printed "Sandy" on a dark green base glass. Patch is yellow. 11/16" in diameter. Jamie Kummer collection.
Above left: "Moon" is the second hardest to find comic in standart comic selection. A "Moon" on turquoise base glass is super rare. The patch is red. Print is in excellent condition. 11/16" in diameter. Jamie Kummer collection.

Above right: This is a "Bimbo" on yellow base glass. The patch looks to be green. It is not clear from this picture if the character is printed on the yellow patch or vice versa. 11/16" in diameter. Jamie Kummer collection.
Above left: A very rare turquoise based glass "Betty". The print seems to be in excellent condition. The patch is red. 11/16" in diameter. Jamie Kummer collection.

89

8-COMICS & ADVERTISING

Above right: An example of a pale green based comics. This is "Sandy". The patch is mustard yellow, which seems to be typical color of choice for this base glass. 11/16" in diameter. Jamie Kummer collection.

Above left: A "Moon" on pale green base glass with mustard yellow patch. Excellent quality print. 11/16" in diameter. Jamie Kummer collection.

Above right: An "Annie" on pale green base glass. The patch could be seen as mustard yellow. Nice quality print. 11/16" in diameter. Jamie Kummer collection.

Above left: This is "Betty" on pale green base glass. The patch color cannot be identified from this picture but one could guess it is mustard yellow. 11/16" in diameter. Jamie Kummer collection.

8-COMICS & ADVERTISING

Above right: A "Skeezix" on pale green base glass. The patch color is not seen from this angle. The print is in excellent condition. 11/16" in diameter. Jamie Kummer collection.
Above left: This is "Koko" on a pale green base glass. The patch is mustard yellow. 11/16" in diameter. Jamie Kummer collection.

Above right: A "Herbie" on green base glass. The patch is yellow. Nice print. 11/16" in diameter. Jamie Kummer collection.
Above left: An "Emma" on pale green base glass. Mustard yellow patch. The print is exceptional. 11/16" in diameter. Jamie Kummer collection.

8-COMICS & ADVERTISING

Above right: "Coat's Master Loaf" is a special promotional advertising piece that is very hard to find. This example has an exceptional print on a harder to find golden yellow base glass and a red patch. 11/16" in diameter. Jamie Kummer collection.

Above left: A "Smitty" on a dark green base glass. The patch is yellow. The marble and the print both are in exceptional condition. 11/16" in diameter. Jamie Kummer collection.

 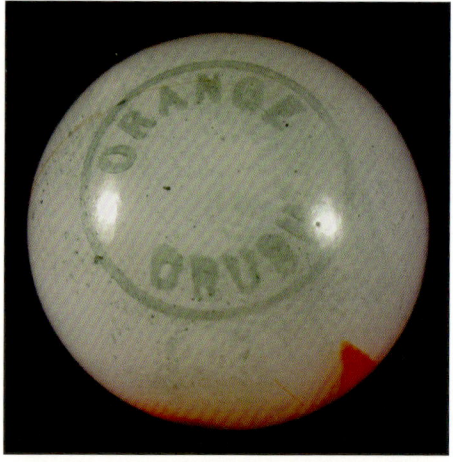

Above right: This advertising promotional piece is almost one of a kind. This one is even rarer than the rarest. The "Orange Crush". The base is translucent moonie white and the patch is red. 11/16" in diameter. Jamie Kummer collection.

Above left: Here is another rarity which the collectors always try to find. A "Tom Mix" on a yellow base glas. The print is superb and the patch is green. 11/16" in diameter. Jamie Kummer collection.

8-COMICS & ADVERTISING

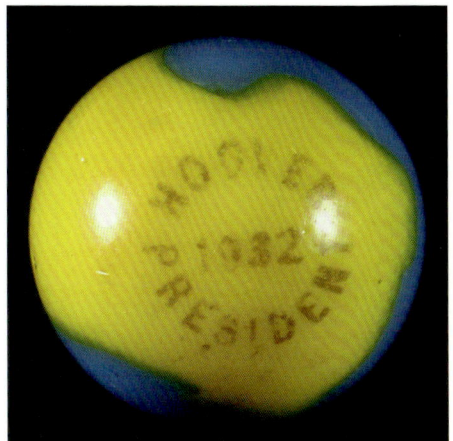

Above right: This is a rare "Tom Mix" with unusual colors. The base is custard yellow and the patch is red. This marble was surfaced in Seattle marble show in late 2010 and made it's way to Ottawa to Jamie's collection. Print and the marble seems to be in excellent condition. 11/16" in diameter. Jamie Kummer collection.
Above left: This is a presidential advertising example of "Hoover" for 1932. This marble was sold on Running Rabbit auction in 1998 and then later found it's way to Ottawa. 23/32" in diameter. Jamie Kummer collection.

Above right: Here is another super rare advertising marble of "Cote's Master Loaf". The colors are white base glass and green patch. The print is in excellent condition so is the marble itself. 11/16" in diameter. Jamie Kummer collection.
Above left: Another "Cote's Master Loaf" on custard yellow base glass with red patch. Condition of the print and the marble seems to be perfect. 11/16" in diameter. Jamie Kummer collection.

8-COMICS & ADVERTISING

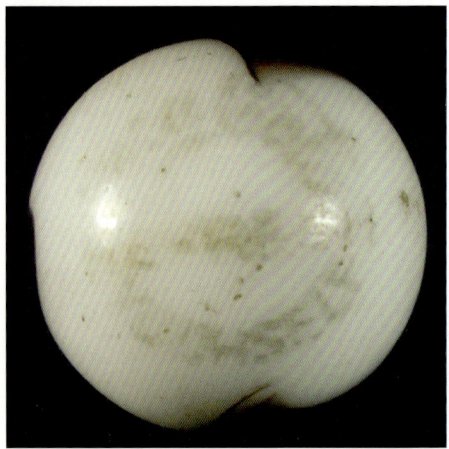 

Above right: A strong and quality print is clarly visible on this super rare Cote's Master Loaf" advertising comic marble. The base is white glass and the patch is red. 11/16" in diameter. Jamie Kummer collection.
Above left: This is a super rare "Coca Cola" advertising marble by Peltier glass. Too bad the print is not as strong as one would like to have, but the rarity makes it up for it. 21/32" in diameter. Jamie Kummer collection.

Above right: It has been mentioned that "Kayo" is already rarest among the standard comic marbles. This one is on a dark green base glass with a yellow patch. A very rare and desirable comic. 11/16" in diameter. Jamie Kummer collection.
Above left: A "Tom Mix" on a white base glass with a red patch. Print is decent. 11/16" in diameter. Jamie Kummer collection.

8-COMICS & ADVERTISING

Above right: An "Andy" on a dark green base glass with yellow patch. Dark green is more desirable then lighter green version and this one is a winner. 11/16" in diameter. Jamie Kummer collection.
Above left: The same marble as on the right with a slight difference. The print landed on the yellow patch. Could it be the intent to make the print more visible? 11/16" in diameter. Jamie Kummer collection.

Above right: This is "Smitty" on a dark green base glass. Print is centered on the green so that the patch is not even visible. Peltier preferred to use white base glass to make the prints visible, which made these dark green examples very rare marbles. 11/16" in diameter. Jamie Kummer collection.
Above left: A "Tom Mix" on a white base glass and blue patch. Both the print and the marble itself looks to be in excellent condition. 11/16" in diameter. Jamie Kummer collection.

8-COMICS & ADVERTISING

Above right: This is an "Emma" on a dark green base glass. The patch looks to be yellow. The print is very strong and in excellent condition. 11/16" diameter. Jamie Kummer collection.
Above left: This is a "Herbie" in rare colors. The base is dark green glass and the large patch is yellow. The marble and the print are both in excellent condition. 11/16" in diameter. Jamie Kummer collection.

Above right: This is a "Koko" on dark green base glass. The patch is yellow. The print is a little faded on this very rare example. 11/16" in diameter. Jamie Kummer collection.
Above left: A "Skeezix" on a dark green base glass with yellow patch. Print has minor fading. 11/16" in diameter. Jamie Kummer collection.

8-COMICS & ADVERTISING

Above right: A "Betty" on dark green base glass with an exceptional print. The patch color is not visible on this shot. 11/16" in diameter. Jamie Kummer collection.
Above left: An "Annie" on a dark green base glass. Just as the picture on the right, this one has an exceptional print. Patch color is not visible. 11/16" in diameter. Jamie Kummer collection.

Above right: A super rare "Moon" on green base glass. Patch looks to be yellow. The print is a bit faded but still a very desirable marble. 11/16" in diameter. Jamie Kummer collection.
Above left: A "Sandy" with a super strike on a green base glass. 11/16" in diameter. Jamie Kummer collection.

8-COMICS & ADVERTISING

Above right: This is "Andy" wth very rare colors. The base is dark green glass and the patch is yellow. The strike is in very good condition. 11/16" in diameter. Jamie Kummer collection.

Above left: A "Bimbo" on a dark green base glass. Print has minor fading but still in great condition. Patch looks to be yellow. 11/16" in diameter. Jamie Kummer collection.

Above right: Turquoise base comics are much harder to find than green examples. This is "Andy" on a turquoise base glass. The patch is red. The strike is in very good condition. 11/16" in diameter. Jamie Browder collection.

Above left: A rare "Kayo" in rare colors. This example has a dark green base glass and a large yellow patch. The strike is printed on green perfectly. 11/16" in diameter. Jamie Kummer collection.

8-COMICS & ADVERTISING

Above right: This is "Bimbo" on a super rare turquoise base glass. The strike is in exceptional condition and so is the marble. The patch is yellow. 11/16" in diameter. Jamie Browder collection.

Above left: A rare "Kayo" on a rare color. Base is turquoise and the patch is red on this extraordinarily rare marble. The strike is almost perfect. 11/16" in diameter. Jamie Browder collection.

Above right: Two extraordinarily rare advertising marbles. One is "Hoover For President 1932" and the other is "1933". Strikes are both unfortunately faded on these hard to find marbles. 11/16" on the right, 21/32" on the left marble. Hansel De Souza collection.

Above left: A "Smitty" on a turquoise base. The patch is yellow. The strike is superb. 11/16" in diameter. Jamie Browder collection.

99

RARITIES

Above: This is "Green Lantern". Superhero names are often used by collectors to name Peltier marbles and the names stick for easy identification. Although it is not the intent of this book to promote names in a wide range fashion, we feeel this one deserves recognition. A rare green base National Line Rainbo with black ribbons loaded with aventurine. There is a trace of yellow between couple of black ribbons that could be seen towards the right on the marble. 11/16" in diameter.

    Peltier Glass produced marbles a long time, thus producing a wide range of different in style and quality along the way. This book concentrates in the early years of the production and there are some unique, unusual and rare marbles that collectors are always fascinated and always on the hunt to find. Why these marbles are so rare? Glass might be in limited availability, or the glass compatibility might have posed a problem in production. We may never know.

9-RARITIES

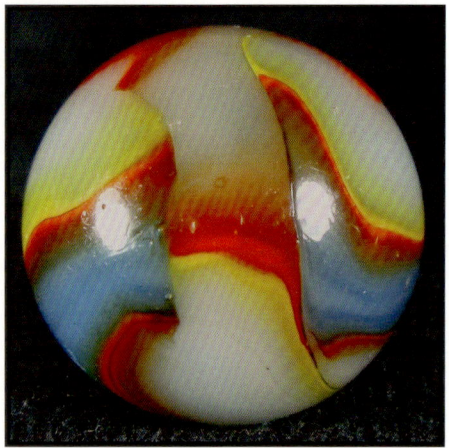 

Above right: This example is in the "Green Lantern" family with the difference of having purplish ribbons rather than black. The ribbons are loaded with aventurine. Collectors named this example "Green Goblin". 11/16" in diameter. Chuck Garrett collection.
Above left: This unusual Peltier marble has translucent white base glass with blue, red and a little bit of bleeding yellow. Quite colorful and hard to find. Chuck Garrett collection

Above right: This is a "Green Rebel". Mint green and black aventurine ribbons swirling on a white base glass. This type of marble typically found in smaller sizes at 5/8" and smaller. We believe this was a short run with limited glass availablity or glass compatibility problems. Chuck Garrett collection.
Above left: At first look this marble looks like a "Bumble Bee", but it is different. The glass looks just like "Green Lantern" glass. We call this one a "Yellow Lantern". Custard yellow base glass with bronze, black or brown aventurine ribbons. Chuck Garrett collection.

9-RARITIES

Above right: This is a "Blue Panther". Black ribbons on a dark rich powder blue base glass. The ribbons typically contain very little to no aventurine. The blue is very different than the turquoise we know Peltier used with the standart production marbles. Chuck Garrett collection.
Above left: This is in the multicolor family with an extra color. Orange, green, blue and white ribbons on a transparent green base glass. Not many can be found.

Above right: One of the highly sought after, classic marble; "Blue Galaxy". Black aventurine ribbons with yellow ribbons on a turquoise base glass. These marbles were always found in smaller 5/8" in size and the pattern most of the time is a swirly pattern. A short run no doubt. We can only guess glass compatibility was the reason Peltier didn't produce many of these. Bill Bass collection.
Above left: A "Green Rebel" with a swirl. Black aventurine ribbons and green ribbons on a white base glass. Bill Bass collection.

9-RARITIES

Above right: This is almost one of a kind example of a "Burnt Brown Bumble Bee". Brown ribbons loaded with brown aventurine on a dark burnt brownish yellow base glass. A super rare bird for sure. 23/32" in size. Kevin Plummer collection.
Above left: This is another example of "Blue Panther". Black ribbons create a wonderful contrast on a dark powder blue base glass. 21/32" in size. Kevin Plummer collection.

Above right: This is a "Green Lantern", a marble every advanced Peltier collector wants to own. It is not only rare but also very beautiful. 11/16" in size. Kevin Plummer sollection.
Above left: A gorgeous example of a "Blue Bee". For some reason Peltier didn't produce too many of "Blue Bees". Blue aventurine could be too expensive for a standart production, but in todays collecting world this one is very highly sought after marble among Peltier collectors. 11/16" in size. Kevin Plummer collection.

9-RARITIES

Above right and left: Two shots of the same marble. This is the elusive "Gray Coat". It is technically a Burnt Liberty with grey ribbons laying on top of the red ribbons on a white base glass. These marbles typically found in larger sizes at arounda, ¾" and larger. Kevin Plummer collection.

Above right and left: Two different shot of two different "Green Lanterns". Both examples show a wide space on the green base that is highlighted with a yellow. Almost twin sisters. Both 11/16" in size. Both Kevin Plummer collection.

105

9-RARITIES

Above right: Two shots of the same marble. This extra rare specimen is also a Lantern family with custard yellow base and red ribbons loaded with aventurine. 21/32" in diameter. Dana and Mark Forrester collection.

Above right: This is a "Yellow Lantern" with the custard yellow base glass and brownish ribbons with aventurine. 11/16" in size. Chad Klein collection.
Above left: Here is another rarity that every collector wants to own. A "Chocolate Cow". It is not clear if Peltier intentionally produced brown based marbles but maybe it wasn't popular with the children, they are not many around. Dark brown base glass with black aventurine ribbons. Collectors are looking for darker shades of brown but the key is the marble shouldn't have any orange or reddish shade. Should be absolute brown to qualify as a "Chocolate Cow". 5/8" in size. Dana and Mark Forrester.

9-RARITIES

Above right: A group of very rare Peltier marbles. Clockwise top is a Yellow Lantern", a Superman", A Green Lantern", A "Green Rebel", a "Copperhead", which is a later Rainbo, a "Blue Galaxy", and two unnamed marbles. Charles Williams collection. Above left: A gorgeous example of a "Green Lantern". 11/16" in diameter. Chad Klein collection.

 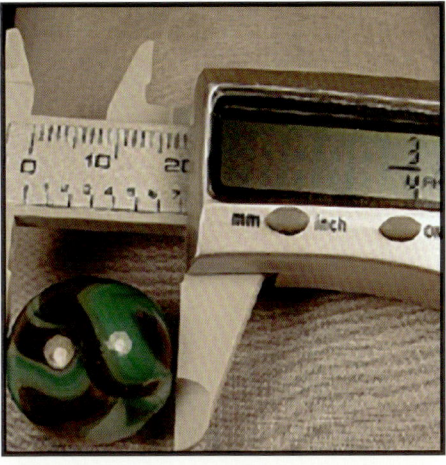

Above right: This example is a rarity among the rarities. "Green Rebels" are always found in small sizes, but this treasure measures a solid ¾" in diameter. Mint green and black ribbons that are loaded with aventurine on a white base glass. Larry and Kathy Runyan Swacina collection.

107

9-RARITIES

Above right: This is a "Green Lantern" with a beautiful pattern. Two cutlines close to each other and the yellow patch is visible to the right. 11/16" in size. Clyde Tuller collection.

Above left: This is a "Burnt Rebel", but the ribbons look to be orange. So it is a "Burnt Orange Rebel". A wonderful swirl pattern. Charles Williams collection.

Above right: A verity of a "Green Rebel". The ribbons are brown with aventurine instead of black. Collectors might have a special name for it and it deserves one. Clyde Tuller collection.

Above left: This is a "Green Goblin". Not a very well known name for a rare Peltier because it is very rare. Same green base glass as a "Green Lantern", but the ribbons are purple instead black and loaded with aventurine. 11/16" in size. Clyde Tuller collection.

9-RARITIES

Above right: This one has black aventurine that are loaded with flashy aventurine on a green base glass. Similar to a "Lantern", but different green glass and no yellow patch. 11/16" in diameter.

Above left: A rare "Dragonfly". It is a mystery why Peltier in early years didn't produce more blue on green marbles, but they did a few. This one is one of them. ¾" in diameter.

Above right: This is a "Brown Bee". Yellow base glass that is the same type of glass that is found with "Blue Panthers", and brown ribbons loaded with aventurine. These marbles typically found in larger 11/16" in sizes.

Above left: Here is a sleeper that is not found every day. This is a "Brown Panther. Same dark powder blue base glass, but brown ribbons instead of black. 11/16" in diameter.

9-RARITIES

Above right and left: Here is a comparison between Brown and Blue Panthers. Original name came from the marble on the left. Powder blue base with black ribbons. The marble on the right was discovered later and named to associate with the marble on the left. It is a "Brown Panther". There could be other color combinations with this base glass. 21/32" on the left marble and 11/16" on the right.

Above right: This is another example of "Green Lantern". Green base glass with four black ribbons loaded with aventurine and a wider space between the ribbons that contain some yellow highlights. 11/16" in diameter.
Above left: A "Chocolate Cow". Four black ribbons loaded heavily with aventurine on a dark brown base glass. 21/32" in diameter.

9-RARITIES

Above right: Another example of a fine "Chocolate Cow". This one has a nice offset ribbons configuration and a beautiful dark brown base glass. There has been some examples found with green aventurine, so check your marbles carefully. 11/16" in diameter.
Above left: This one is a "Blue Bee" with an exceptional pattern. You can see three cutlines on one shot. Beautiful blue ribbons loaded with blue aventurine on a lemon yellow base glass. 21/32" in diameter.

Above right: An interesting example of "Brown Panther". Brown ribbons on a somewhat darker than normal powder blue base glass. The marble almost looks like a West Virginia swirl, but it is a Peltier. 11/16" in diameter.
Above left: This is a "Blue Bee". Four blue ribbons loaded with blue aventurine on a lemon yellow base glass. The yellow base always have a different shade and texture on "Blue Bees". The glass type might be a shortly available glass, which would explain why these marbles are so rare. 11/16" in diameter.

111

9-RARITIES

Above right and left: Two shots of the same marble. Here is a marble that is not easily to be found. This is a "Yellow Goblin". Purplish red ribbons that are loaded with aventurine on a custard yellow base glass. This marble is no doubt is in "Green Lantern" family. 11/16" in diameter.

Above right: This unusual marble has brown ribbons swirling with a ying yang pattern and end up on a cutline on a green base glass. Could be named a "Pistaccio". Ying Yang pattern shot could be viewed on page 155. 11/16" in diameter.
Above left: This is a "Chocolate Cow" with a lighter shade of brown base. Collectors value darker shade of brown bases more, but this one is so brown it is ranks high up in the rarity factor. This one has a gorgeous offset ribbon configuration. 11/16" in diameter.

9-RARITIES

Above right and left: two examples of colorful National Line Rainbos. Both marbles have a base glass that is half and half different colors. Sometimes called as "Bifurcated" to discribe the type of marble. Half blue and the other half green base glass. Ribbons vary from red to brown. Both marbles 11/16" in diameter.

Above right: This is a Miller "Blue Wasp". Any Wasp with blue aventurine is very hard to find but with a pattern like this is extra hard. 11/16" in size. Kevin Plummer collection.
Above left: This marble feels like it belongs to the late period of National Line Rainbos when the transition to later Rainbos started; circa late 1930'ties. It has yellow ribbons on a green base glass. 11/16" in diameter.

9-RARITIES

Above right: This is a gorgeous "Cubscout" on a bifurcated base glass. Half of the base is turquoise and the other half is green. Bright yellow ribbons finish the colorful scheme. 11/16" in diameter.
Above left: A special multicolor. There are white, green, salmon and blue ribbons on a transparent green base glass. An additional color makes this example a rare "Salamander". 11/16" in diameter.

Above right and left: Two shots of the same marble. Here is the holy grail of a Peltier collection; A "Grey Coat". Technically it is only a Burnt Liberty, but the combination is so pretty collectors gave it a special name. Grey ribbons lay on top of red ribbons on a white base glass. There are Burnt Liberties that did not grey out and also Grey Coats that the ribbons do not lay on top of each other to make things more confusing. This marble is in 13/16" in diameter.

114

9-RARITIES

Above right: This is a highly sought after bifurcated Spiderman. Half of the base color is turquoise and the other half is green. Ribbons are red. The extra third color in this type of examples makes these marble very colorful and collectors want one in their collection.

Above left: This is a rare bifurcated "Dragonfly". Half of the base glass is a gorgeous blue and the other half is white. The ribbons are green. Not many are found consistently. This one is 23/32" in diameter.

Above right and left: Two shots of the same marble. This is a magnificent "Golden Rebel". The pattern is beautifully balanced whereever you turn the marble. The rich red ribbons makes this one so attractive. 13/16" in diameter.

115

TRANSPARENT & TRANSLUCENT NLRS

Above: This is a "Green Submarine". Submarines are very limited production and not many are found to make a strong assesment of the types and available color selection. This one has transparent green base glass with orange ribbons and yellow highlights. The cutlines are close to each other and create a fantastic pattern. One of the best Peltier marbles we have ever seen. 11/16" indiameter.

    Early Peltier National Line Rainbo marbles were thought as opaque base with two or three color ribbon marbles. That is absolutely not correct. Peltier produced magnificent marbles with transparent and translucent base glass. We want to cover as much as possible through some of the best examples we were lucky enough to photograph and present to the reader.

10-TRANSPARENT & TRANSLUCENT NLRS

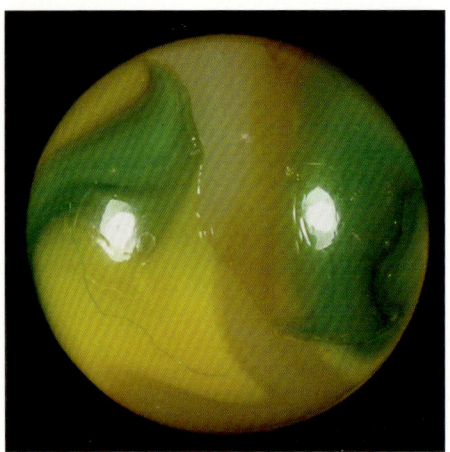 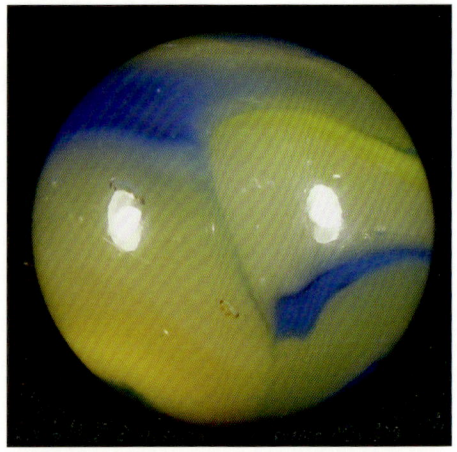

Above right: A "Blue Angel" needs to have a translucent base glass, a blue and yellow ribbons running between two cutlines. The base is preferred to have a muddy color. The darker the tan base color the more valuable the marble is. Chuck Garrett collection.
Above left: A "Green Angel" has the same configuration except it has green instead blue ribbons. Quite attractive eye appeal on these marbles. They most likely belong to the late National Line Rainbo period when the production started to shift towards later Rainbo line. Chuck Garrett collection.

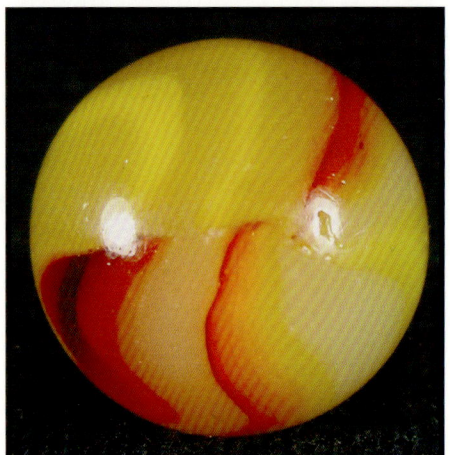 

Above right: This is a "Green Fizz". Green and white ribbons on a bubble filled clear base glass. This is a very pretty marble that got into collectors radars recently and the values go up faster than any other Peltier marble. 11/16" in size. Chuck Garett collection.
Above left: This is a "Red Angel". Red and yellow ribbons on a translucent base glass. 5/8" in size. Chuck Garrett collection.

10-TRANSPARENT & TRANSLUCENT NLRS

Above right: This is a "Fruit Cocktail". This National Line Rainbo marble has four ribbons with four different colors on a clear base glass. This example has blue, red, yellow and white ribbons. Charles Williams collection.
Above left: Another "Fruit Cocktail" with a ying yang pattern. There are three, two and one color version of Fruit Cocktails. Chuck Garrett collection.

Above right: Here is another blue, red, yellow and white "Fruit Cocktail" on clear glass. 11/16" in diameter.
Above left: This combo has a green ribbon replacing the blue. These marbles are highly sought after by collectors because they are early and very colorful. Sizes range from 5/8" to ¾". Charles Williams collection.

119

10-TRANSPARENT & TRANSLUCENT NLRS

Above right and left: This is an example of "Silver Surfer". White and black aventurine ribbons on a green tinted transparent base glass. The base glass is bubble filled. The white ribbons cover most of the marble except a small window area, where one could view inside the marble. A wonderful specimen. 21/32" in size. Chuck Garett collection.

Above right: Here is a gorgeous example of "Blue Angel". Blue and yellow ribbons on a translucent muddy base glass. These marbles are believed to be produced in a late National Line Rainbo period. Kevin Plummer collection.
Above left: Here is a "Green Angel". Green and yellow ribbons on a translucent muddy base glass. Green Angels are somewhat harder to find than Blue Angels and Red Angels. Kevin Plummer collection.

10-TRANSPARENT & TRANSLUCENT NLRS

Above right and left: Two shots of the same marble. This is a "Blue Surfer" swirl marble. Blue ribbons which contain aventurine most of the time and white filaments swirl between couple of cutlines on a blue or green tinted transparent base glass. Aventurine is not too heavy and one might need to check with a loupe to identify it. This one is 11/16" in diameter. Kevin Plummer collection.

Above right and left: Two shots of the same marble. Here is a very hard to find Peltier National Line Rainbo marble. This example has black aventurine ribbons with yellow and white ribbons on a clear base glass. 5/8" in diameter. Kevin Plummer collection.

10-TRANSPARENT & TRANSLUCENT NLRS

Above right and left: Two shots of the same marble. Here is another unusual and hard to find National Line Rainbo marble. This example has black aventurine ribbons with red and white ribbons on a clear base glass. 5/8" in diameter. Kevin Plummer collection.

Above right: This is a translucent Ketchup & Mustard. Red and yellow ribbons running between two cutlines on a translucent white base glass. There is a thin green ribbon which makes this a very rare hybrid example. 5/8" in size. Chad Klein collection. Above left: A hard to find red transparent National Line Rainbo. Four red ribbons running between couple of cutlines on a clear base glass. 23/32" in size. Dana & Mark Forrester collection.

10-TRANSPARENT & TRANSLUCENT NLRS

Above right: This is a "Green Fizz". White ribbons swirling and running between couple of cutlines on a bubble filled, transparent light green base glass. These marbles could have been made during late period of NLR era. Charles Williams collection.
Above left: Here is a superb example of a "Submarine". Orange ribbons running between couple of cutlines on a transparent, almost maglight blue base glass. There are Submarine examples with green base glass also. 5/8" in size. Chad Klein collection.

Above right: This rare Peltier has red, black and white ribbons on a clear base glass. It is not understood why clear base NLRs are harder to find and rare. One alternate thought might be that the company was thinking that these are not as attractive to kids as much as the opaque marbles. Charles Williams collection.
Above left: Another clear based National Line Rainbo with yellow, black and white ribbons. Charles Williams collection.

123

10-TRANSPARENT & TRANSLUCENT NLRS

Above right: This is a "Submarine". Dark red ribbons running between couple of cutlines on a maglite transparent blue base glass. There is a little whispy white in there too that is visible when backlit. Clyde Tuller collection.
Above left: A magnificent "Silver Surfer". These type of swirl marbles are thought to belong to early production as they are very rare, beautiful and the glass is somewhat different. This marble has white and black aventurine ribbons on a green tinted transparent base glass. Dani & Ernie Kirk collection.

Above right: This example looks like it belongs to a Multicolor family, but there is a difference. This one has only green and red ribbons and the base glass is clear rather than green tinted typical to Multicolor swirls. Regardless, it has a gorgeous pattern and size.
Above left Here is another "Submarine" with a little darker, brownish ribbon. Cutlines are close to each other. 11/16" in diameter. Chad Klein collection.

10-TRANSPARENT & TRANSLUCENT NLRS

Above right: A "Green Angel" with green and yellow ribbons on a muddy translucent base glass. 11/16" in size. Clyde Tuller collection.
Above left: A "Blue Angel" with blue and yellow ribbons. This example does not have a muddy base but still looks good. 21/32" in size. Clyde Tuller collection.

Above right: This marble is a close relative to "Fruit Cocktail" family with blue, red and white ribbons on a clear base glass. A three color "Fruit Cocktail". 11/16" in diameter.
Above left: A very unusual Peltier marble. This one does not have a name yet but definitely deserves one. White and green ribbons, almost blending, on a translucent muddy base glass. 11/16" in diameter.

125

10-TRANSPARENT & TRANSLUCENT NLRS

Above right: A three color "Fruit Cocktail" with red, yellow and white ribbons on a clear base glass. This one represents a ¾" size also.
Above left: A four color "Fruit Cocktail" with green, red, yellow and white ribbons on clear base glass. A very colorful combination. 11/16" in diameter.

Above right: This marble would be a two color "Fruit Cocktail" with yellow and white ribbons on a clear base glass. The marble has a wonderful ying yang pattern. 21/32" in diameter.
Above left: This rare and unusual marble has pale yellow, blue and white ribbons on a green tinted transparent base glass. Probably an early attempt for a Multicolor swirl. 11/16" in diameter.

10-TRANSPARENT & TRANSLUCENT NLRS

Above right: An example of a "Liberty Citrus". These marbles typically have two colors and whispy white on a translucent base glass. Liberty Citruses have a distinctive orange ribbons replacing the classic red. This one is 11/16" in diameter.
Above left: Another "Liberty Citrus" with orange, blue and whispy white ribbons. Translucent base could be seen through the small window. 11/16" in diameter.

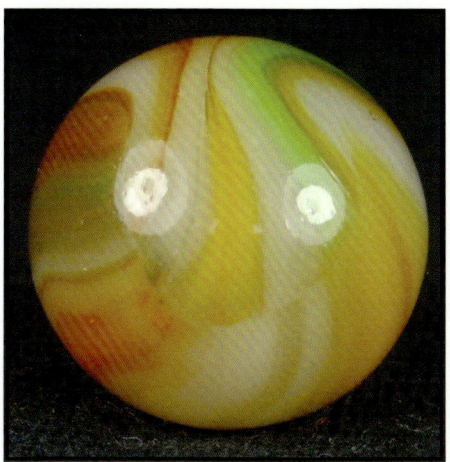 

Above right: A very popular among Peltier marble collectors is the "Plum Citrus". This marble is unique on its own because it has the only purple ribbon in all early Peltier marble production. Purple, yellow and whispy white on translucent base glass. 11/16" in diameter.
Above left: This is the "Citrus" itself. A very colorful marble with green, yellow with some orange highlights and whispy white on a translucent moonie base glass. 11/16" in diameter.

127

10-TRANSPARENT & TRANSLUCENT NLRS

Above right: Another gorgeous example of the "Citrus". This one has also green, yellow, a little orange and whispy white. The pattern on these marbles are typically straight with minor swirling. 11/16" in diameter.
Above left: A "Plum Citrus" with purple, yellow and whispy white ribbons. A gorgeous classic ribbon layout. 11/16" in diameter.

Above right and left: Two shots of the same marble. This is a four color "Fruit Cocktail". Classic color combination of green, yellow, red and white on a clear base glass. Two cutlines and straight ribbon configuration. 11/16" in diameter. These types of marbles are believed to have been produced early National Line Rainbo period and sizes were from 5/8" to ¾" in diameter.

10-TRANSPARENT & TRANSLUCENT NLRS

Above right: A rather rare early Peltier marble. This example has orange and white ribbons on a transparent cobalt base glass. 11/16" in diameter. Sami Arim collection. Above left: A three color "Fruit Cocktail". This one has two yellow, one red and one white ribbons on a clear base glass. Ribbons go deep into the marble. A classic beauty for sure. 11/16" in diameter. Sami Arim collection.

Above right: Four white ribbons swirling between couple of cutlines on an emerald green transparent base glass. The pattern is absolutely gorgeous. 11/16" in diameter. Above left: Four thick yellow ribbons running between couple of cutlines on a rare transparent yellow base glass. This color combination is very hard to find. 11/16" in diameter.

129

10-TRANSPARENT & TRANSLUCENT NLRS

Above right: White ribbons swirling wildly on a transparent emerald green base glass. Green base is more common than any other color we have seen in this type of Peltier NLR swirl. 11/16" in diameter.
Above left: Four wide green ribbons running berween couple of cutlines on a clear base glass. We have seen this type with blue, red, white, turquoise and yellow ribbons as well. 11/16" in diameter.

Above right: White ribbons swirling on a transparent smoky teal blue base glass. Cutlines are lined up close to each other for a nice pattern. 21/32" in diameter.
Above left: Six white ribbons running between couple of cutlines on a transparent olive green base glass. 11/16" in diameter.

10-TRANSPARENT & TRANSLUCENT NLRS

Above right: Four white ribbons on bright emerald transparent base glass. 21/32" in diameter.
Above left: Another white ribbons on transparent green example. These type of marbles were found typically larger 11/16" in diameter and most of them boost a nice pattern. This one is 11/16" in diameter too.

Above right: This marble has four white ribbons on a brilliant transparent red base glass. Just like the green examples, these are found in larger sizes from 11/16" to ¾" in diameter. This one is 11/16" in diameter.
Above left: Four white ribbons on a transparent darker red base glass. 11/16" in diameter.

131

10-TRANSPARENT & TRANSLUCENT NLRS

Above right: This marble is a "Green Fizz". Probably belongs to late NLR to early Rainbo period. White ribbons on a bubble filled transparent light green base glass. 11/16" in diameter.
Above left: Another pretty marble which most likely belongs to early Rainbo time period. White ribbons with a little bit of yellow swirling on a translucent light blue base glass. 11/16" in diameter.

Above right: Four white ribbons on a transparent red base glass. The pattern is classic four ribbon configuration. 11/16" in diameter.
Above left: Four gorgeous turquoise ribbons running between two cutlines on a clear base glass. 21/32" in diameter.

10-TRANSPARENT & TRANSLUCENT NLRS

Above right: Opposite of the marble on the previous page, this one has white ribbons on a bubble filled transparent turquoise base glass. The pattern of these types are most of the time found as very swirly. 11/16" in diameter.
Above left: Four yellow ribbons that are wide and deep into the marble running between two cutlines on a clear base glass. 11/16" in diameter.

Above right: This is a gorgeous 4 to 6 white ribbons on a transparent bubble filled red base glass National Line Rainbo. This example is very similar to contemporary Mexican Vacor examples, but the cutlines and the rest of the pattern shows the difference. 21/32" in diameter.
Above left: This is a Peltier swirl with a very hard to distinguish classic Peltier pattern. Blue and white ribbons swirling all around on a green tinted base glass. Some of these show more transparent base and some of them show some aventurine. We call it a Fancy Peltier swirl. 11/16" in diameter.

10-TRANSPARENT & TRANSLUCENT NLRS

Above right: This marble has white ribbons running between cutlines on a maglight translucent red base glass. The base glass does not show any transparency without the back light. 11/16" in diameter.
Above left: Four wide and thick ribbons running between two cutlines on a crystal clear base glass. This marble has the green ribbons found in Fruit Cocktails, so this is a one color Fruit Cocktail. 11/16" in diameter.

Above right: A six ribbon transparent National Line Rainbo. 6 white ribbons running between two cutlines on an olive green transparent base glass. Ribbons run deep into the marble and show the structure of typical NLR configuration. 11/16" in diameter.
Above left: Another 6 white ribbon NLR on transparent amber base glass. The verity of color selection, the beautiful colors makes these marbles very desirable among collectors. This marble is 11/16" in diameter.

10-TRANSPARENT & TRANSLUCENT NLRS

Above right: A "Blue Angel" with white translucent base glass. Hard core collectors look for a muddy brown base to classify these marbles as "Blue Angels".
Above left: This is a "Blue Submarine". Orangish red ribbons running between two cutlines on a maglite blue base glass. The contrast of the colors are just stunning. In addition this marble has aventuine in the red ribbons. 11/16" in diameter.

Above right: Another "Submarine" with the similar colors as the previous example. It is hard to see the tranparency of the base glass without the back lighting. Ribbon colors varies from dark brownish red to bright orange on these examples. Aventurine is a big plus.
Above left: Another blue based "Submarine" except this one has yellow ribbons. Only blue and green 'Submarines" have been classified as "Submarines" up to this book print. This one is 11/16" in diameter.

10-TRANSPARENT & TRANSLUCENT NLRS

Above right: This is an unusual and hard to find National Line Rainbo. It has bubble filled clear base glass and 4 ribbons just like a regular two color NLR. However, this marble technically has three colors if you count the clear base as a third color. Ribbon colors are a dead match to "Dragon" colors, so it is safe to call it a "Clear Dragon". *Above left:* A late National Line Rainbo swirl which has been a collector's favorite hunting subject a long time. It is very hard to find example of "Green Angel". It has a translucent muddy brown base glass with green and yellow ribbons between cutlines.

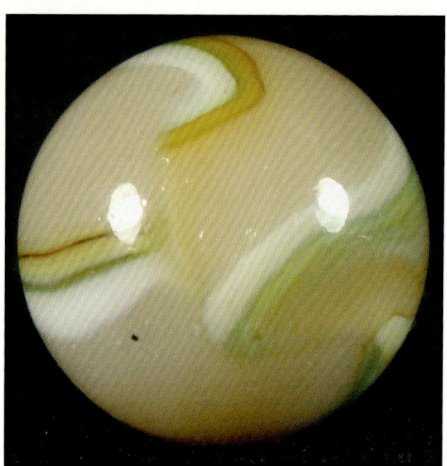 

Above right: This is a "Blue Lagoon" or a "Blue Surfer". Blue, and white ribbons swirling on a blue tinted transparent base glass. Chuck Garett collection.
Above left: A translucent muddy base glass with green, white and brown ribbons. Mark & Dana Forrester collection.

10-TRANSPARENT & TRANSLUCENT NLRS

Above right and left: This extraordinary early Peltier clear based marble was found in Ohio Canton show in 2013. I named it as "Orange Crush". The marble has 4 to 6 orange ribbons with yellow highlights swirling wildly on a clear base glass. The ribbons dive deep into the marble to give a 3 dimensional depth.

Above right and left: Another "Orange Crush" with a ying yang pattern to add to the masterful design. The marble is ¾" in diameter, typically found in early Miller swirls.

137

AVENTURINE

Above: A magnificent example of what Peltier Glass was able to do in early years of marble production. This example is loaded with bronze aventurine on a light green base glass. The ribbons forming a swirly pattern and the color combination is not very common. The marble is 11/16" in size.

    Aventurine is a type of glass that was dicovered in Italy around mid 17th century. It is sometimes confused with several minerals like quartz or feldspar which also have tiny flecks of glittering material that shine and sparkle. The name itself suggests discovering something by chance, through luck or adventure but even if it was found by accident most likely this special glass making process was passed through generations of family secrets and formulas that was kept secret. Essentially, the glass was combined with copper and copper slats. When the glass melted and cooled these mineral deposits create the sparkly appearance.

11-AVENTURINE

Peltier Glass company was a master in making aventurine glass. The company used this knowledge in their marble production side of the business. Aventurine was used mostly in the early 10-15 years of marble production. Later towards the end of 1930's when production required cost cutting, faster per minute with less rejects, Peltier Glass started using aventurine less and less. Aventurine glass was also more expensive. Aventurine can be found in later Rainbos that were produced in 1940'ties but they are very rare.

Peltier Glass used mostly black aventurine in the marbles. Most commonly they are found in Zebras, Tigers, Wasps, Bumble Bees, and Rebels. They could be found with much rarity in Flaming Dragons, Liberties, Ketchup & Mustards, Christmas Trees and Supermans. Bronze, green, brown and blue aventurine was also used by Peltier and are highly collectible and sought after. Very rare marbles like Silver Surfer, Blue Surfer (Blue Lagoon), Green Lantern, some Submarines are found with aventurine. Hard to find limited production Peltier Glass marbles like Golden Rebels and Blue Galaxies are almost always produced with aventurine.

Any above mentioned Peltier marble could be found with bronze aventurine which is quite harder to find. Brown aventurine has only been seen in Bumble Bees so far but that does not mean they are not present in any other color combinations. They are definitely very rare. Blue aventurine is the most highly sought after type of aventurine in Peltier marbles. Blue Bee, Blue Wasp and Blue Tiger are few examples that are found with this rare aventurine. Green aventurine was found in Green Zebras, Bumble Bees, Chocolate Cows and Tigers. Other types are believed to to be produced with this rare type of aventurine.

Another couple type of hard to find Peltier Glass marbles that may have aventurine are Burnt Christmas Trees and Burnt Rebels. These marbles have been found with aventurine with 50% probability.

Aventurine in Peltier Glass marbles is a very important aspect of collecting Peltier marbles. Although it is not number one factor of falling in love with these marbles but it is definitely one of the more important and desirable factor why collectors love Peltier marbles.

11-AVENTURINE

Above right: This is a "Blue Deer" with green and blue aventurine. Blue aventurine looks to be gathered at the edges of the green ribbons. There seems to be a little spillover to the yellow base glass. 21/32" in size. Chuck Garrett collection.
Above left: This is a second shot of the cover marble. Black ribbons loaded with bronze aventurine and green aventurine over the light green base glass defines this ultra rare example. 11/16" in diameter.

Above right and left: Two shots of the same marble. This is a "Bronze Zebra". Bronze aventurine is loaded on brown ribbons on a white base glass. The ribbons are swirling wildly and what a gorgeous pattern. 5/8" in size. Chuck Garrett collection.

11-AVENTURINE

Above right and left: This marble, as well as most marbles rest of this book should be in the rarity section. But this one is exceptional. This marble has blue and white ribbons loaded with silver aventurine on a green tinted transparent base glass. Too bad there are not many of these out there. Every collector would want one in their collection. Chuck calls this "Dark Universe". Chuck Garrett collection.

Above right: This is a "Blue Bee". Blue Bees are considered among the hard to find classification among early Peltiers. Blue aventurine where it gets thin shows a little green tint. The yellow base on these marbles always show a different lemon yellow base glass, which could means that they are a short lived run. 21/32". Kevin Plummer collection.
Above left: A "Blue Wasp". Even rarer than the Blue Bees", Blue Wasps have blue ribbons with blue aventurine on a red base glass. Bill Bass collection.

142

11-AVENTURINE

Above right and left: This rare specimen definitely deserves a name. Looks to be it could be a distant relative to Multicolor swirls but colors of this marble are completely different. Blue ribbons are loaded with blue aventurine and the base glass is maglite. 5/8". Kevin Plummer collection.

Above right: A "Blue Wasp" showing a thick blue ribbon loaded with azure blue aventurine. Typically Blue Wasps have a red base glass that has a little bit of orange tint to it. A special short lived run for sure. Kevin Plummer collection.
Above left: There are two names for this type of marble. It is either called a "Blue Surfer", associating the marble with its cousin "Silver Surfer", or a "Blue Lagoon", describing the beauty with a nick name. Blue and white ribbons with aventurine on a green tinted transparent base glass. 5/8". Jeff Wichmann collection.

11-AVENTURINE

Above right: A hard to find "Liberty" with blue aventurine. This pose showing the thick, wide blue ribbon that is loaded with blue aventurine. "Liberties" with aventurine are highly sought after by Peltier collectors. This one is 11/16" in diameter. Kevin Plummer collection.
Above left: A "John Deer" with aventurine. This beauty shows green ribbons that are loaded with green aventurine sprinkled all over the marble. And a superb pattern. Kevin Plummer collection.

Above right and left: two shots of the same marble. This exquisite early Peltier marble is called a "Silver Surfer". Black ribbons with aventurine and white ribbons swirling wildly on a green tinted transparent base glass. This example is 21/32" in diameter. Kevin Plummer collection.

11-AVENTURINE

Above right and left: Two shots of the same marble. This is as desirable and beautiful as the previous marble. This is a "Blue Surfer". Blue and white ribbons swirling wildly on a light green or blue tinted transparent base glass. Blue ribbons almost always contain aventurine. 11/16" in diameter. Kevin Plummer collection.

Above right: This magnificent "Wasp" not only has one of the richest dark red base glass we have seen but also has some of the rarest aventurine we have found on Peltiers. It is loaded with silver aventurine. 21/32" in diameter. Bill Tite collection. Above left: A superb example of blue aventurine. This is a "Blue Zebra". Blue ribbons loaded with blue aventurine running and swirling between two cutlines on a white base glass. 11/16" in diameter. Bill Tite collection.

145

11-AVENTURINE

Above right: This "Golden Rebel" is shwoing a very wide black ribbons looking almost like a patch and absolutely loaded with aventurine. Aventurine presence on a Peltier marble makes it very desirable for collectors. Mark & Dana Forrester collection.
Above left: This very unusual and rare marble is probably from "Lantern" family and a close relative to "Yellow Goblin" except the ribbons are not purple but red. Aventurine is spilling over the custard base and looks almost green. 21/32" in diameter. Mark and Dana Forrester collection.

Above right: A magnificent example of a "Brown Zebra". Thick brown ribbons loaded absolutely with brown aventurine running between two cutlines that are close to each other, on a white base glass. A great pattern and a rare marble. Chad Klein collection.
Above left: Another superb example of blue aventurine. This wide ribbons is showing rich blue aventurine on a white base glass. Mark & Dana Forrester.

11-AVENTURINE

Above right and left: A rare marble with an exceptional pattern. This is every Peltier collectors dream marble. A Miller swirl "Blue Wasp". Blue ribbons absolutely loaded with azure blue aventurine swirling wildly on a red base glass. 11/16" in diameter.

Above right and left: This magnificent marble is an exotic "Silver Surfer". Black and white ribbons with aventurine running between two cutlines that are close and parallel to each other on a bubble filled transparent green base glass. This marble shows the difference between the types that they can be very swirly or straight ribbons like this one. The marble is a healty 11/16" in diameter. Clyde Tuller collection.

147

11-AVENTURINE

Above right: This is a rare "Spiderman" with sparkly aventurine at the edges of the red ribbons. A gorgeous marble. 21/32" in diameter. Clyde Tuller collection.
Above left: A "Christmas Tree" with green aventurine ribbons. This rare marble always have the same transparent red and the forest green on white base glass. The green ribbons are loaded with green aventurine. 21/32" in diameter. Clyde Tuller collection.

Above right and left: An almost "Golden Rebel" but not quite. This marble is actually much rarer than a "Golden Rebel". Collectors named this as "Ruby Bee", but this particular example is more than that. Black aventurine tracing the red ribbons almost like a tracer on a golden yellow base glass. 11/16" in diameter. Clyde Tuller collection.

11-AVENTURINE

Above right and left: Another magnificent "Silver Surfer" with black aventurine ribbons and white filaments swirling on a green transparent base glass. A fantastic pattern on this example. Everything about this marble directs us to the early production but we can't be sure. Clyde Tuller collection.

Above right: This is a rare example of "Superman" with aventurine. "Supermans" with aventurine typically show a moderate amount. Regardless it is a very desirable marble. Clyde Tuller collection.
Above left: A third shot of the same "Silver Surfer" above. Whereever you turn the marble there is a superb pattern. Clyde Tuller collection.

149

11-AVENTURINE

Above right: A "Blue wasp" with a blue ribbons loaded with blue aventurine on a red base glass. Clyde Tuller collection.
Above left: This is a "Blue Deer" with blue aventurine on green ribbons. This combination is extremely rare and very desirable. Clyde Tuller collection.

Above right: This is a "Bronze Bee". Brown ribbons loaded with bronze aventurine on a custard yellow base glass. Bronze aventurine can be found on Tigers, Zebras, Wasps etc. This is a nice example. 11/16" in diameter. Clyde Tuller collection.
Above left: A "Ruby Zebra" with aventurine. The ribbons look almost a brownish red and are loaded with aventurine. Clyde Tuller collection.

11-AVENTURINE

Above right: This is a very unusual marble for Peltier Glass. It is a Multicolor swirl with aventurine. Aventurine sprinkled all around the marble and not concentrated on a single ribbon. We have seen only couple examples like this. Mustard yellow, turquoise and white ribbons on transparent green tinted base glass. 11/16" in diameter.
Above left: This is a "Bronze Tiger". The black ribbons are loaded with bronze aventurine on an orange base glass. Bronze aventurine is not found very often on Peltier marbles. This one is 11/16" in diameter.

Above right and left: This is a "Blue Lagoon" or "Blue Surfer". Whichever the name is the marble is magnificent. Blue and white ribbons swirling wildly on a green tinted transparent base glass. 11/16" in diameter.

11-AVENTURINE

Above right: This is a "Christmas Tree" with aventurine. This type of Christmas Tree is not very common. It always have the same forest green and transparent red ribbons. Green ribbons on this example is absolutely loaded with aventurine. A special run for sure. 11/16" in diameter.

Above left: A rare "Green Surfer". Green and white filaments swirl wildly on a transparent base glass. Green ribbons contain moderate amount of aventurine on the poles where the ribbon make a loop. 11/16" in diameter.

Above right and left: Two shots of the same marble. This is a "Ruby Bee". Four red ribbons running between couple of cutlines on a golden yellow base glass. The red ribbons are loaded with aventurine. There is a separate orange line as a bonus on this beautiful marble. 11/16" in diameter.

12-YING YANG PATTERN

YING YANG PATTERN

Above: A "Bronze Bee" with a ying yang pattern. Bronze aventurine is a hard to find type of aventurine to find on any marble. That is the same for Peltier marbles. It is found mostly on Bumble Bees and sometimes on Tigers. This one also have a very desirable pattern. 11/16" in diameter. Sami Arim collection.

    This pattern is found in almost all type of marbles that are made throughout the history. But no company ever made so many marbles with it. Peltier Glass seems to create this pattern at will and marbles with this pattern are highly sought after among Peltier collectors. The pattern basically makes a handgathered swirl at one pole and then creates a "V" and returns to either ending as regular ribbons on the cutlines or rarely goes the other pole and creates another circling swirl. Double ying yang swirls are called "Ram's Head" pattern and are very desirable.

12-YING YANG PATTERN

Above right: A "Superman" with a ying yang pattern. Ribbons are not blended and created a clean colorful pattern. A magnificent specimen. Bill Bass collection.
Above left: This is a "Fruit Cocktail" with a ying yang pattern. It is not clear if Peltier created this pattern at will or it was just a result of their machinery. Regardless, they produced many of these patterns. 21/32". Chuck Garrett collection.

Above right: A magnificent "Blue Bee" with a ying yang pattern. Blue ribbons loaded with blue aventurine are swirling beautifully on a yellow base glass. Chad Klein collection.
Above left: This looks to be a "Tiger" with ying yang pattern. There are some blends and beautiful design. Kevin Plummer collection.

12-YING YANG PATTERN

Above right: This is a "Flaming Dragon" with a ying yang swirl. Orange ribbons with some yellow highlights on a green base glass. Superb pattern that every collector is looking for. Clyde Tuller collection.
Above left: This is white on transparent red NLR swirl with the pattern. Charles Williams collection.

Above right: A very unusual color combination for Peltier. Brown ribbons swirling on a pistachio green base glass. Other side of the marble is shown on page 112 to show the offset ribbon configuration. 11/16" in diameter.
Above left: A "Flaming Dragon" with the ying yang swirl. Orange ribbons with yellow highlights on green base glass. 11/16" in diameter.

12-YING YANG PATTERN

Above right: This is a transparent NLR swirl. Green ribbons on a clear base glass. The pattern is gorgeous. 11/16" in diameter.
Above left: This pattern mostly found on Multicolor swirls and this is one example. Salmon, blue and white ribbons on a green tinted base glass. 23/32" in diameter.

Above right: White ribbons on a bubble filled transparent red base glass. A beautiful example with a gorgeous pattern. 21/32" in diameter.
Above left: White ribbons on a transparent green base glass. There is a little bit of brown mixed, but the pattern is great. 11/16" in diameter.

12-YING YANG PATTERN

Above right and left: Two shots of the same marble. This is an aqua feathered slag. Beautiful pattern and size. White filaments swirling on a transparent aqua base glass. This is a perfect example of a Ram's Head with both sides having the swirl. Third pictures is below. 11/16" diameter.

Above right: This is a "Bumble Bee" with a ying yang pattern. Nice swirling pattern with a balanced ribbon layout. 11/16" in diameter.
Above left: Third picture of the above marble. Two poles have the swirling pattern and this shot is from the middle. 11/16" in diameter.

12-YING YANG PATTERN

Above right and left: This is a bifurcated "Spider-Dragon". Half marble has turquoise and other half has a green base glass. Red ribbons swirling beautifully all around. Some nice blending of colors give extra characteristics to the marble. 11/16" in diameter.

Above right: This is a Hybrid "Burnt Christmas Tree". There is red and burnt brown ribbons with some burnt green on white base glass. The pattern is nice.
Above left: A magnificent example of Miller "Rebel" with a ying yang pattern. The marble is already very hard to find but with this pattern it is superb. ¾" in diameter.

12-YING YANG PATTERN

Above right: This is a "Blue Panther" with a ying yang pattern. Black ribbons rarely contain aventurine on these. The blue base is a different shade than the usual turquoise Peltier Glass typically uses. 5/8" in size. Jeff Wichmann collection.
Above left: This is a Liberty with a fantastic ying yang pattern. Transparent blue and red ribbons swirling on a white base glass. 23/32" in size. Jeff Wichmann collecton.

Above right: This is a red slag with a ying yang pattern. White filaments swirling on a transparent red base glass. This example is about ¾" in size. Jeff Wichmann collection.
Above left: This rare specimen has cream and a little bit of blue lines swirling on a transparent red base glass. 23/32" in size. Jeff Wichmann collection.

159

SLAGS

Above: A fetheared red slag with a wonderful pattern. Featheared white filaments formed a little thicker on this example looking almost like ribbons. The base glass is a transparent red. 23/32" in diameter.

Slag type marbles were some of the earliest type of marbles that were produced by Peltier Glass Company. Slag type marbles typically are white thin ribbons swirling on colored transparent base glass. They are also called as Onyx marbles. The examples of early years of Peltier Glass Company slags are not categorized or in other words not clearly distinguished from other companies' slag marbles unless they have a very typical Peltier pattern on them. Peltier Glass however has produced a very typical type of slag that is different than any other companies' slag type marbles. It is called "Fetheared Slag". It has white ribbons swirling between couple of cutlines.

13-SLAGS

Above right: This is an "Aqua Slag" with a fantastic pattern. It is not clear from this angle if the marble has any ying yang pattern, but looks like it may have a Ram's Head pattern. White filaments on a brilliant aqua base glass. 11/16" in diameter.
Above left: This is a fetheared green slag. White filaments swirling wildly on a transparent green base glass. The pattern on this example is simply gorgeous. White filaments give a darker look towards the surface of the glass. 11/16" in diameter.

Above right: This is a green slag with white fetheared white filaments looks like a tree on a transparent green base glass. 11/16" in diameter.
Above left: Another example of a green slag. Green base glass looks to be a little darker than the previous example. Fetheared white filaments run wildly on a transparent green base glass. 11/16" in diameter.

13-SLAGS

Above right: This is a fetheared red slag. Red slags are thought to be harder to find compared to other colors, but vaseline and white are probably the most difficult colors to find. This red slag has a beautiful pattern and a nice size at ¾" in diameter.
Above left: A purple slag. Probably the most elegant color among the fetheared slag selection, this example is showing a gorgeous pattern. 11/16" in diameter.

Above right: This is a fantastic example of Peltier Glass Fetheared Slag marble. White ribbons on transparent cobalt blue base glass. Sometimes the white ribbons gather on one side of the marble and form this pattern. 5/8" in size. Bill Bass collection.
Above left: Another superb example of a red slag. White filaments meet at two cutlines that are very close to each other on a transparent red base glass. This is also a huge example at ¾" in diameter.

163

14-ORIGINAL PACKAGING

ORIGINAL PACKAGING

Above: A colorful example of Peltier National Line Rainbo original box. The cover shows some Art Deco design with colorful circles and lines mimicking marbles. The marbles are all three color National Line Rainbos circa 1930's. 10 each Liberties, Ketchup & Mustards, Rebels and Christmas Trees. Marty Ruhland collection.

Antique and vintage toy, marble or any other collectible has much more value if it is in original box they came in. Marble collectors value original packaging very highly not only because the marbles would be in best condition, which is not necessarily a correct statement, but it also gives marbles a provenance and credibility as their origin. Peltier Glass Company sold marbles in many colorful original packaging starting with Gropper & Sons in early years and later with their own name only. We tried to show some of the best examples of Peltier Glass Company original packaging examples in the book to represent the veriety and colorful design of these boxes.

14-ORIGINAL PACKAGING

Above: A magnificent original box of Peltier Glass National Line Rainbo box with 3 color NLR and some selection of character marbles. There are 4 Supermans, Rebels, Christmas Trees, Ketchup & Mustards, possibly Liberties in this box. Note all character marbles are different and thus gives the impression of being original to the box. Although they could be carefully backfilled with the individual comics without duplication it does not matter at this point whether or not if they are indeed original to the box. Yellow based comics are additionally a bonus. From Marthy Ruhland collection.

14-ORIGINAL PACKAGING

Above: Same box cover as the previous page. Although there is some minor damage at the corners the box overall is in excellent condition. The Indian chief head and Indian motives on the bands on both sides of the chief are gorgeous. Company name and address id printed on the side of the box. Marty Ruhland collection.

14-ORIGINAL PACKAGING

Above: A fantastic box of complete set of character marbles. There is a yellow example of this box existing also. Cover shows the print "Collect Them All", which tells us these marbles were collected from the moment they hit the shelves and still very collectible today. Marthy Ruhland collection.

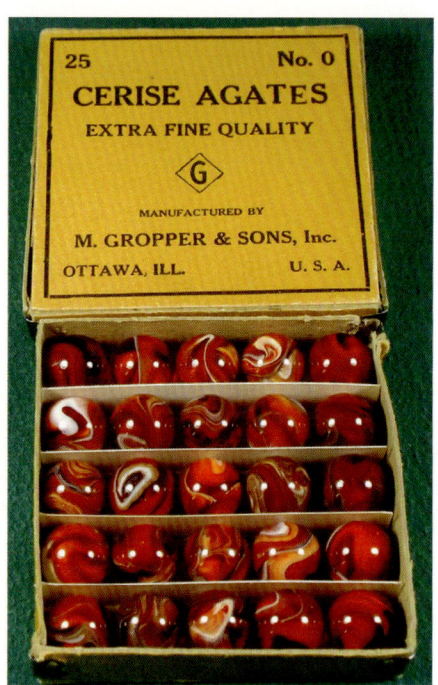

Left: This is an early original packaging example with M. Gropper & Sons were the sole distributor of Peltier marbles up until 1931. Marbles are examples of early Peltier red slags which do not show fethearing characteristics but easily could be confused with Akro Agate slags if they are not in this particular box. A superb example of early Peltier Glass Company handgathered slags in original box. Marty Ruhland collection.

168

14-ORIGINAL PACKAGING

Above: A gorgeous Art Deco design cardboard box of 3 color National Line Rainbos with a black leather pouch. This piece could also qualify for an advertising item with colorful centerpiece. There seems to be 5 each K&M, Rebel, Superman, Christmas Tree and Liberty 3 color marbles with an additional marble at the column to the right. Below: A closer shot of the cover. A very colorful cardboard cover with triangular motifs and an advertising design in the center. Marty Ruhland collection.

14-ORIGINAL PACKAGING

Above: A National Line Rainbo box with two color NLRs. 5 each with 4 columns. First column are Red Bees. After that is a line of Zebras, Red Zebras, and Cubscouts. Below: A collection of National Line Rainbo boxes. Marty Ruhland collection.

14-ORIGINAL PACKAGING

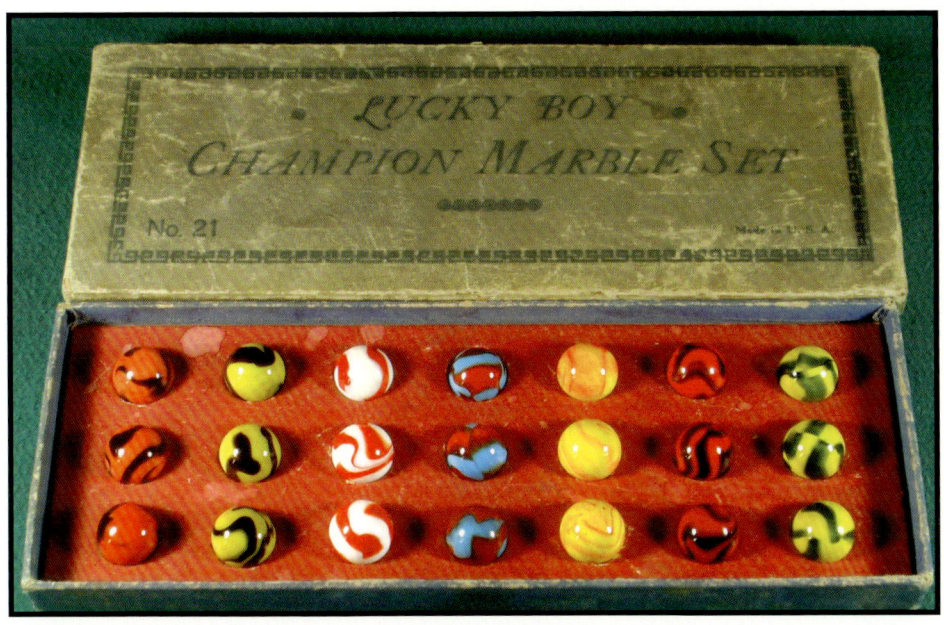

Above: A rare cardboard box of Lucky Boy box with No 21 printed on it. Marbles are all two color NLRs; three each Tigers, Bumble Bees, Red Zebras, Spidermans, Red Bees, Wasps, and John Deers.
Below: Another carboard box of Lucky Boy box with 3 color NLRs. Marty Ruhland collection.

14-ORIGINAL PACKAGING

Above: A beautiful 32 count Lucky Boy box in excellent condition. The box is blue on the exterior with red interior. This example has all feathered slags that are most of the time found in this type of boxes. There are 4 of each color example of slags in this box. Marty Ruhland collection.

14-ORIGINAL PACKAGING

Above: A 40 count National Onyx Marbles" cardboard box. There are two rows each different color including two rows of aqua, two rows of blue, two rows of green, two rows of purple and one row each red and white slags. These marbles were called as Onyx marbles those days and maybe collectors should be calling them as such today. Vaseline color is missing in this box. It is an early box showing Gropper logo. Marty Ruhland collection.

14-ORIGINAL PACKAGING

Above: This is a beautiful grey jobber box filled with single color clear based National Line Rainbos. This type of early NLRs do not get much attention but they are definitely very pretty and deserve more credit. In addition to these colors there are white, and red examples as well as tinted transparent based ones known. Marty Ruhland collection.

Below: A little original comic box that holds 5 comic marbles. This one shows which comics are included on the cover and it is in excellent condition. Jamie Kummer collection.

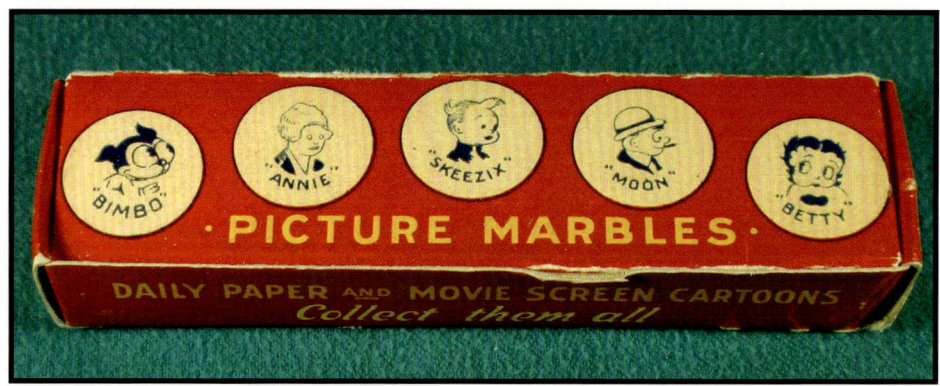

174

14-ORIGINAL PACKAGING

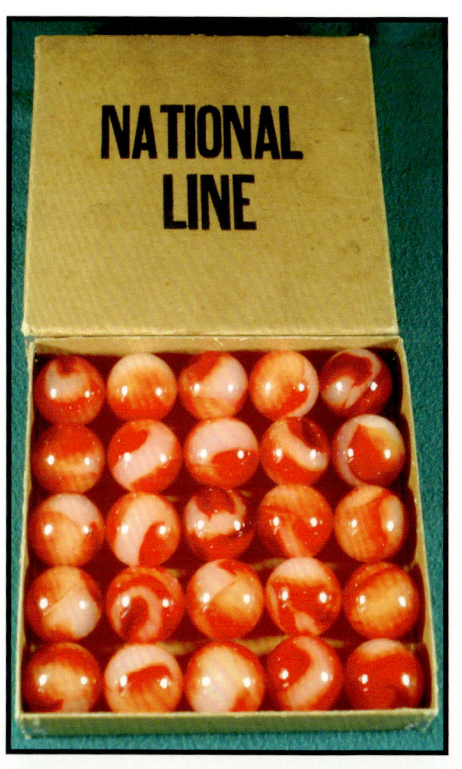

Left: A National Line Rainbo cardboard box filled with two color NLRs. The marbles appear to have red ribbons with a translucent silver base glass. Marty Ruhland collection.

Below: This is a 100 count cardboard box filled with Rainbo marbles. There is a print on the side that says National Line but the marbles are a generation later types. The marbles are all white base Rainbos and could have easily been backfilled since these are much more common and easily found to replace earlier NLRs. Marty Ruhland collection.

14-ORIGINAL PACKAGING

Above: A 24 count early National LIne Rainbo box in amazing pristine condition. The pouch and the marbles seems to be all original to the box and are also in excellent condition. The marbles are a mixture of two and three color National Line Rainbos with one row of red on white patch marbles. It is also an advertising piece. Marty Ruhland collection.

14-ORIGINAL PACKAGING

Above: This is a magnificent 100 count National Line Rainbo cardboard box. There is a mixture of two and three color NLR marbles in the box with three colors being Ketchup & Mustards and a column of Christmas Trees. First column is Dragons, third are Cubscouts, Zebras, Red Bees, Tigers, Spidermans, Red Zebras, and Flaming Dragons as two Color NLRs. Marty Ruhland collection.

14-ORIGINAL PACKAGING

Above: A very similar box to the previous page. The box and the marbles are from the same time frame except these are all patch marbles. These are called Peerless Patches and they are marked as such at the top of the box. Peerless Patches are typically the type of marbles with a single ribbon on top of a white, yellow, green or turquoise base glass. These are the type of marbles that are also used for Character marbles. Marty Ruhland collection.

14-ORIGINAL PACKAGING

Above: This is an early 100 count Peltier Glass cardboard box filled with white feathered slag marbles. Collectors always question if Peltier actually made white slag marbles and if they did they are very rare. They are indeed rare but there are 100 of them here in this box. Marty Ruhland collection.

179

14-ORIGINAL PACKAGING

Above and below: A gorgeous 28 count Lucky Boy box filled with feathered slag marbles. Marty Ruhland collection.

14-ORIGINAL PACKAGING

Above: An early Gropper cardboard box filled with slag marbles. It cannot be confirmed if the marbles are Akro Agate or Peltier marbles. Marty Ruhland collection. Below: A large size jobber box with 35 count National Line Rainbos. Marty Ruhland collection.

181

14-ORIGINAL PACKAGING

Above: A colorful cardboard box filled with unusual set of National Line Rainbo marbles. First and third columns clearly showing some Citrus family Liberty and Christmas Trees. Second column appears to be a clear K&M. Third and fifth columns are some kind of hybrid NLRs with Christmas Tree colors. Marty Ruhland collection.
Left: An unusual design on the cover of this box. The marbles date to 1940's so must be the box. All marbles belong to Tracer family and have a translucent moonie base glass. Tracers are a generation later Rainbos and named for a white ribbon tracing a second color on a translucent base glass. In this case second colors are green, blue, yellow and red. Marty Ruhland collection.

14-ORIGINAL PACKAGING

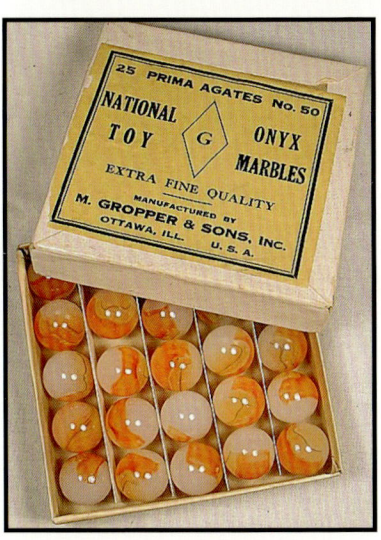

Above: A fantastic colorful Art Deco cover with two color National Line Rainbos. Top row are Zebras, second row are Lemon-Lime (or John Deer), third row seems to be Wasps or Tigers, fourth row Bumble Bees and bottom row are Red Zebras. Marty Ruhland collection. Left: A beautiful example of Gropper & Sons box marked as "Prima Agate" at the top. Marbles are called Honey Onyx and do not display early Peltier characteristics. These marbles typically have an orange patch on a translucent moonie base glass. These marbles are mostly in larger 11/16" to ¾" in size. They are very collectible and not easy to find. Charles Williams collection.

14-ORIGINAL PACKAGING

Above: A beautiful Art Deco box with blue, red, grey and white stained glass designs. The pouch is solid green. Hansel de Souza collection.
Below: An exceptionally rare group of turquoise based comic marbles. Patches are red or yellow in this super rare collection. One comic is missing which is "Sandy". Jamie Browder collection.

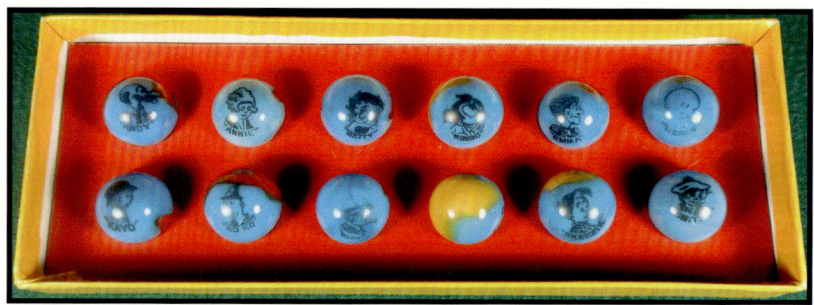

14-ORIGINAL PACKAGING

Above: A magnificent orange jobber box with all yellow based comic marbles filled with it. Patches alternate as red or green in this examples. Jamie Kummer collection. Below: A grey jobber box filled with extremely rare examples of comic and character marbles. Note five "Cotes Master Loaf" advertising examples all white base glass, couple of Tom Mix character marble, one with blue patch and the second with an unusual orange patch on white base glass. Rest of the marbles are in rare green base glass with yellow patches. Some examples have stamped on the yellow patch. Overall a super rare group. Jamie Kummer collection.

14-ORIGINAL PACKAGING

Above: A red jobber box filled with white base glass comic marbles. Patches are red, blue, green, black colors.
Below: A complete set of red comic box with bonus "Cotes" and "Tom Mix" shown with the rest of the group. Patches appear to be all red in this collection. Jamie Kummer collection.

14-ORIGINAL PACKAGING

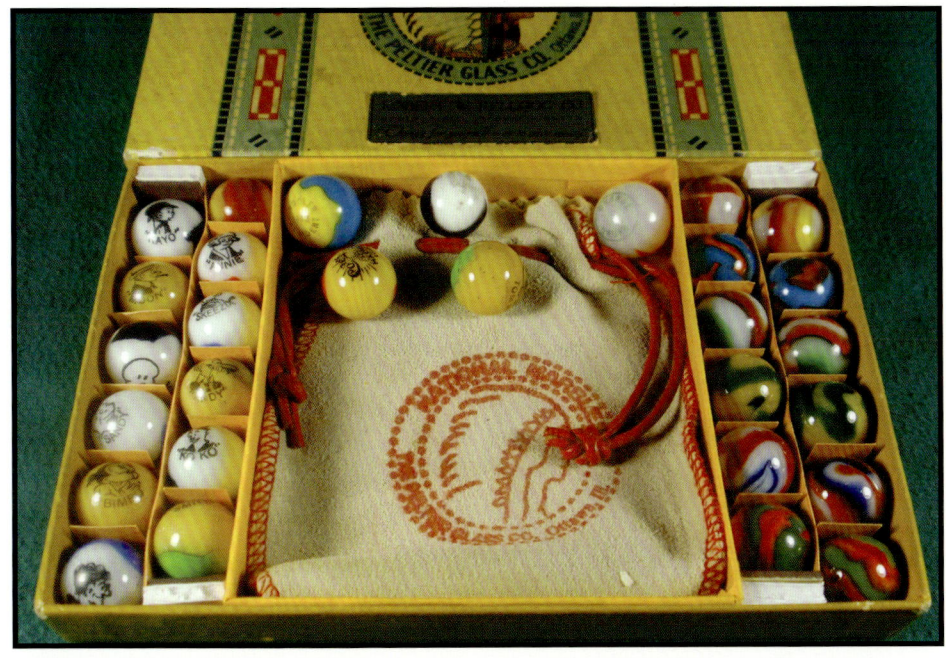

Above and below: An outstanding example of Peltier box filled with rare character marbles and National Line Rainbos. The box looks to be in fantastic mint condition as well as the pouch and the marbles. Jamie Kummer collection.

187

14-ORIGINAL PACKAGING

Above: A yellow original comic box filled with light green based comic marbles. One example might be a yellow based or the stamp could be on the patch. Couple examples appear to have darker green base. Jamie Kummer collection. Below: A Lucky Boy box in exceptional condition. Charles Williams collection.

14-ORIGINAL PACKAGING

Above: A yellow box with bottom cardboard portion replaced with a wood box to provide strength. The set is complete and the marbles are all different combinations. Bob Hutchison collection.
Below: Another example of the same combination. Yellow top with wood bottom and white base character marbles. Bob Hutchison collection

14-ORIGINAL PACKAGING

Above: A complete set of comic marble collection on a contemporary wooden box. Bob Hutchison collection.
Below is a nice yellow original box in great condition. Charles Williams collection.

100
NATIONAL ONYX
Manufactured by
M. GROPPER & SONS, Inc.,
TOY MARBLES
No. 0
NEW YORK, N. Y. U. S. A.

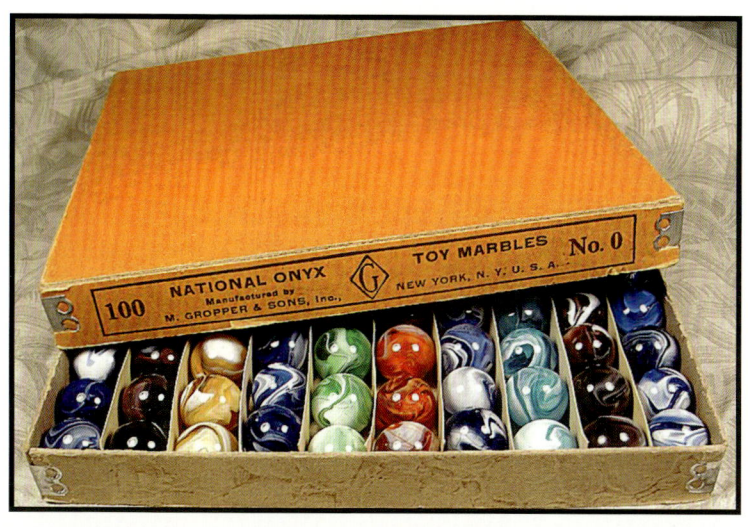

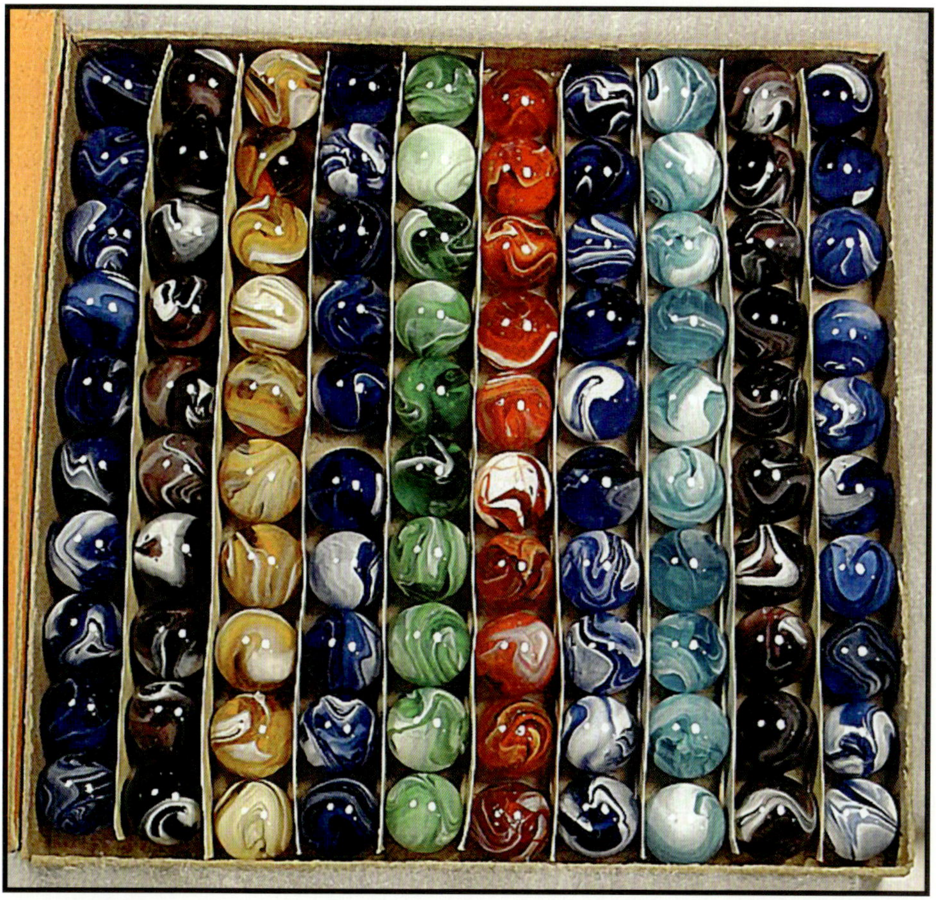

14-ORIGINAL PACKAGING

14-ORIGINAL PACKAGING

NO. 224 NATIONAL MARBLE SET

Above: Cover of a NLR box. Box is in excellent condition. Charles Williams collection.
Below: An interesting print on the pouch in this example. Charles Williams collection.

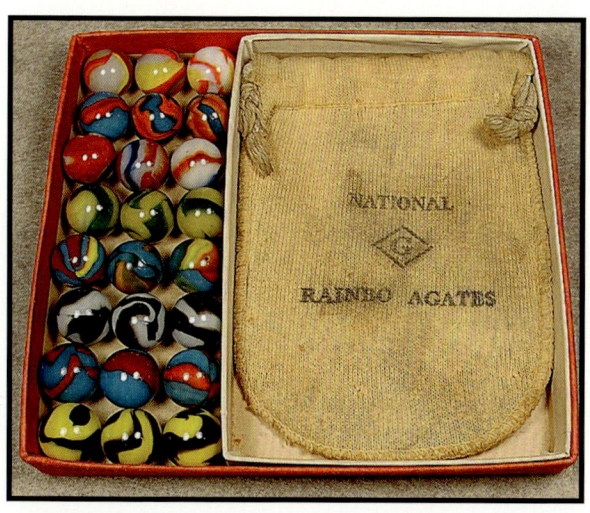

193

14-ORIGINAL PACKAGING

Above is a 20 count National Line Rainbo box.
Below is a small 5 count comic box. Both from Charles Williams collection.

14-ORIGINAL PACKAGING

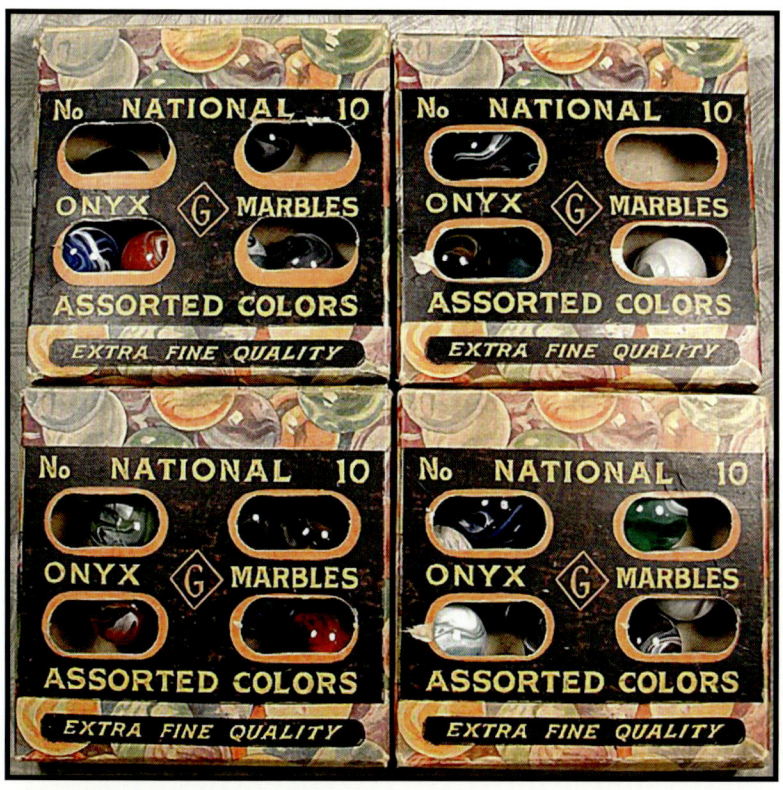

14-ORIGINAL PACKAGING

14-ORIGINAL PACKAGING

Previous page: A 100 count 1940's Rainbo box with 100 white based Rainbos. Ribbons are all the same in every column which is a good indicator of marbles being original to the box. Charles Williams collection.
Above: An absolutely gorgeous Art Deco tiled cardboard box of 15 National Line Rainbos. Marbles are all two color Rainbos. The box and the pouch seems to be in fantastic condition. An early 25 count "Cerise Agate" red slag box with M. Gropper & Sons print.

14-ORIGINAL PACKAGING

Above: An early Gropper & Sons Cerise Agate box. Hansel de Souza collection.
Below: This was sent to us as a Peltier pouch. The marbles are mix match and look to belong to late NLR period. Hansel de Souza collection.

14-ORIGINAL PACKAGING

Above: A 100 count alternating red on white and green on white Peerless Patch marbles. The base glass might be translucent on these marbles. Next page: Another 100 count Peerless Patch cardboard box. This example has additional couple of columns with yellow on white, black on white and blue on white patches. Note the three color example at the bottom of black on white marbles. Hansel de Souza collection

14-ORIGINAL PACKAGING

200

14-ORIGINAL PACKAGING

Above: A very early 25 count Prima Agate box with Gropper & Sons print. These marbles are very much the same marbles that are found in Christensen American Agate boxes and collectors are confused as to what exactly to believe. One important note is that there are Christensen Agate examples found with stripes and cutlines that are easily identified as Christensens and these marbles do not show classic ribbons and cutline configuration early Peltier Glass marbles show. Hansel de Souza collection.

14-ORIGINAL PACKAGING

Above: A very important box in exceptional condition. This is a National Line Rainbo era box with two and three color marbles. There is one trio of translucent patch marbles in there. Box is a brilliant red carboard. Hansel de Souza collection.
Below: A fantastic example of Peltier Glass National Line Rainbo box. On the left are two and three color National Line Rainbo swirls and on the right are a set of comic marbles. The red pouch does not show a print but there is no reason why it would not be original to the box. It seems to be in excellent condition. Next page above: A colorful Art Deco cover with three color National Line Rainbos and original leather pouch. Note the beautiful green pouch does not show any print regarding Peltier Glass Company. Next page below and the following page: This is a card board box containing 6 box of 5 count comic marbles. It is important to note that the boxes are all the same character marbles. Peltier Glass Company called these marbles "Picture Marbles". Hansel de Souza collection.

14-ORIGINAL PACKAGING

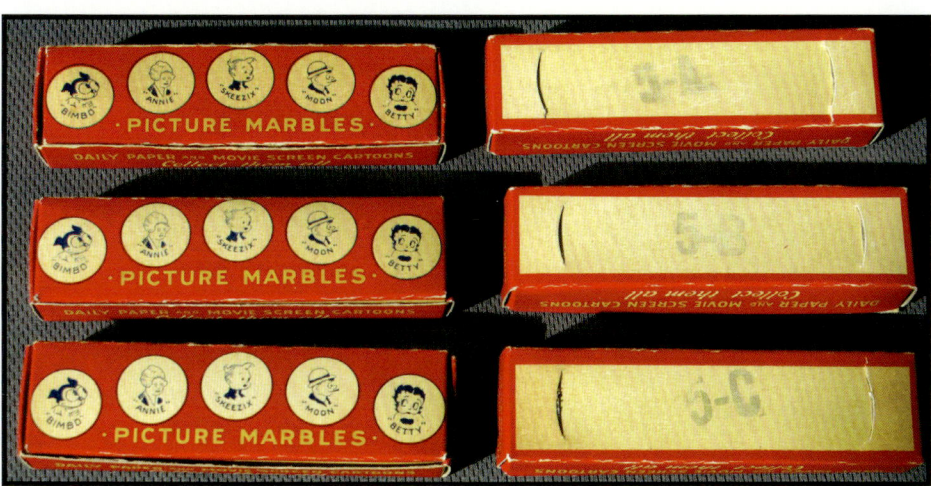

203

62-7901
PICTURE MARBLES
2 DOZEN
PICTURE MARBLES
No. 5
THE PELTIER GLASS CO.
OTTAWA, ILLINOIS

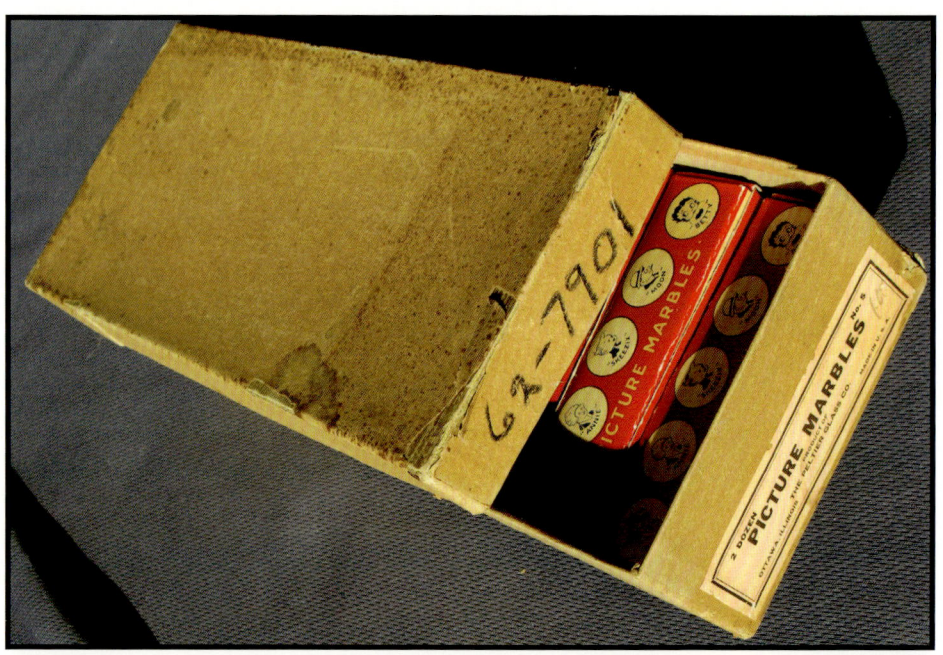

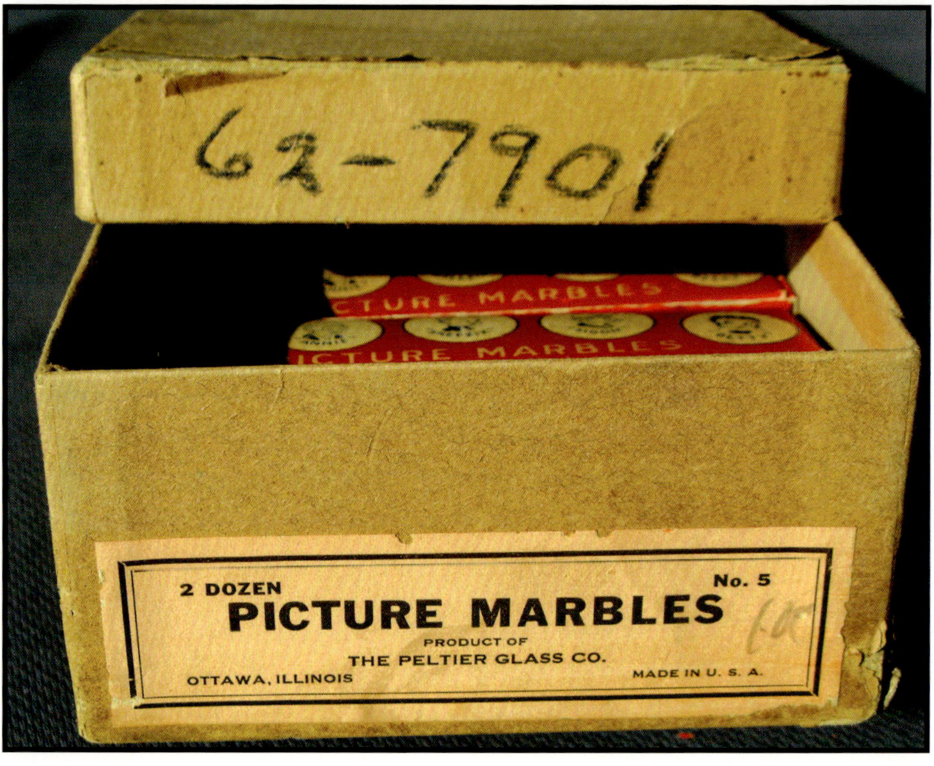
62-7901
PICTURE MARBLES
2 DOZEN
No. 5
PICTURE MARBLES
PRODUCT OF
THE PELTIER GLASS CO.
OTTAWA, ILLINOIS
MADE IN U. S. A.

14-ORIGINAL PACKAGING

Above: A 25 count National Line box. The identification National Line Rainbos are for the period of late 1920's to late 1930's marble production. With that understanding this box should have early National Line Rainbos. The marbles in this box looks like they are a generation later Rainbos all white base glass with different color ribbons. Hansel de Souza collection.

14-ORIGINAL PACKAGING

Above: A circa 1940's Rainbo cardboard box an probably earlier advertising box. Green marbles are probably Master Glass. There seems to be couple of West Virginia swirls backfilled in the boxes. Left box is showing a Blue Panda while right box is boosting a Liberty and a Spiderman. Hansel de Souza collection.

14-ORIGINAL PACKAGING

207

14-ORIGINAL PACKAGING

Previous page above: A yellow character marble box with a complete set of marbles. Yellow base "Sandy' is probably the rarest and most valuable in the box.
Previous page below: A red example with complete set of marbles. Lower left marble looks like a rare turquoise based "Sandy", but I can't be sure.
Above: An orange jobber box with yellow and white base character marbles. Bob Hutchison collection.

14-ORIGINAL PACKAGING

Above: An Art Deco stained glass designed cover with blue, green, red, yellow and grey colors. This is an unusual 40 count Peerless Patch marbles. Note the red patch on pink examples at the right end of the box.

Next page: A hundred count box of National Line Rainbo marbles. Interestingly the marbles are called as "Sunsets", which today among collectors the name is used for later Rainbos with orange and white ribbons on bubble filled clear base glass. This magnificent box contains all three color National Line Rainbos with one column of Supermans. It is an earlier box with Gropper & Sons Inc. marked on the sides of the box. It is also printed "National Toy Marbles" at one side of the box.

14-ORIGINAL PACKAGING

14-ORIGINAL PACKAGING

Above: A bird's eye view of the 100 count box. Marbles probably were produced right in the heart of early National Line Rainbo circa mid 1930's. Note the red ribbons on some Christmas Trees, Ketchup & Mustards, Rebels and Liberties have a burnt brown cast to it. This group proves that three color National Line Rainbos with red ribbons could come out of the furnace burnt and it doesn't mean a specific time period.

14-ORIGINAL PACKAGING

Above: cover shot of the 100 count box. It is interesting to see "Sunset" printed in between the "National Marbles". We can't be sure if Peltier Glass Company used the naming convention for the three color NLR marbles. It may have been used randomly as needed but today collectors do not associate the name "Sunset" with these marbles. Sunsets are a specific later Rainbos with orange and white ribbons on a bubble filled clear base glass.

14-ORIGINAL PACKAGING

Above: An excellent treasure and a very important clue on how the early Peltier Glass slag marbles looked. Generally slag marbles are easy to distinguish between Peltier Glass feathered slags, Christensen Agate slags and MF Christensen slags. Peltier Glass feathered slags are covered in this book with pictures; Christensen Agate slags have a single or double cutlines with typical lines and colors and so does MFC with mostly a figure "9", a tail ending on a single cutline showing being hand gathered. Marbles above do not show a feathering white lines and they could be easily confused with Akro Agate slags unless carefully studied. Note that there is a column of the controversial Prima Agates that look very much the same as Christensen Agate's "American Agates". How did they get in there? The column with orange slags are probably "Cerise Agates". No reason to doubt if the marbles are original to the box as they very much look to be.

14-ORIGINAL PACKAGING

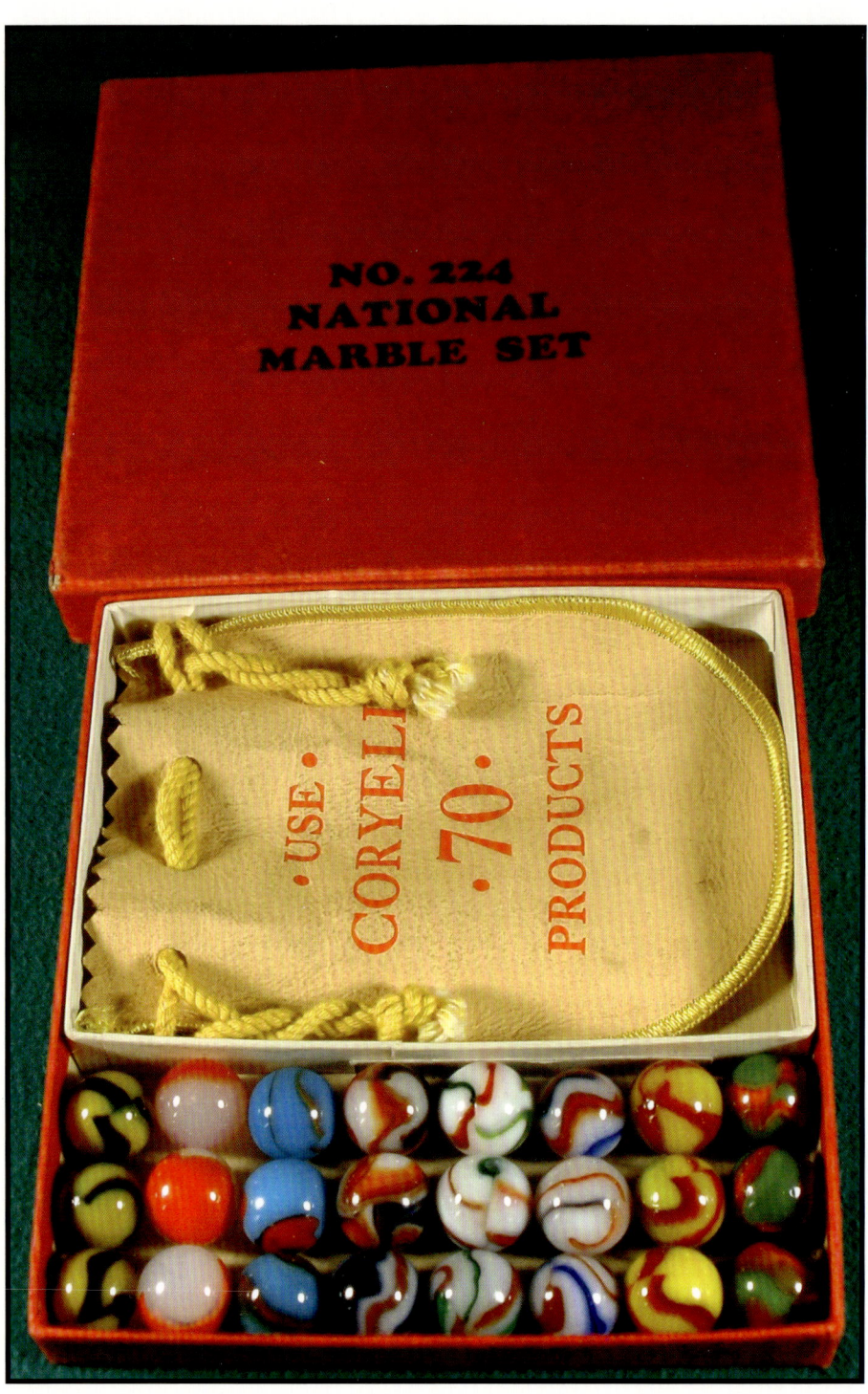

14-ORIGINAL PACKAGING

CONCLUSION

It is the end of this book but by no means the end of the whole story. This book, as intended from the moment the idea developed, concentrated in the early period of Peltier Glass toy marble production. However, the story of Peltier Glass continued for more than a decade into early 1950's. Towards the end of National Line Rainbo production second half of 1930's, the look of the marbles started to change. The standard marble color combinations began to end and different color combinations as well as glass colors were being introduced. It is probably appropriate to call this period a transitional period from the early National Line Rainbos to Rainbos. It is difficult to determine how long this transitional period lasted but it ended with standard Rainbo production that lasted another decade or more. Peltier Glass produced some of the most beautiful and unique marbles during this short period.

Typical identification for Rainbos of the coming decade of 1940's are that they are more standardized in sizes, so there are more 5/8" Rainbos although there are other sizes that can be found. Shooters were also continued and were 13/16" to 1" in sizes. Expensive aventurine glass was no longer used and again, there are Rainbos that contain aventurine but are very rare and because of this rarity are very desirable. Glass quality was also somewhat dropped and became more watery if that is the description. Colors were not as strong, opaque or bright as earlier NLR marbles. Patterns were more simplified, ribbons were more on the surface and the swirling, that Peltier marble collectors love, pretty much was minimized. These changes were most likely made to make the marble production business sustainable so it can continue and make profit. Costs were cut down to compete with all other marble making companies and survive.

The remaining part of Peltier Glass toy marbles needs another in depth study and definitely another book that will complement this book and finish the story of a beloved toy of the past. There is still much to be researched and written about the beginning, the rise and the end of Peltier Glass Company. We hope that this is a good start and as time goes by and more and more passionate collectors dive into the details of the history it will all be revealed in time. But before all of that happens let us all enjoy what we have for now.

16-AUTHOR'S BIOGRAPHY

Sami Arim, born in 1961, holds a bachelor's degree in architecture and currently working as an architect in San Francisco, California. He has been collecting marbles since he was 7 years old and is still going strong. He specializes in Peltier Glass marbles but collects all kind machine made and handmade marbles. He is married to Luciana and has two children Antonio and Ayla.

Michael Johnson, born in 1955, has spent his whole life and career on the Central Coast of California. For thirty-four years he has been teaching various subjects, including History, in both the public schools and in the state prison system. As a historian and researcher he co-authored six books on marble history since 1994. His pride and joy remains forever his two children, Miranda and Jolyon. Photo courtesy of Ashlyn Snow.

Gino Biffany, (1938-2015) born in Ottawa, the Peltier Glass factory hometown. He worked for AT&T for over 40 years. He was a founding member of the Illinois Valley Carver Association and a lifelong Peltier marble collector and historian. He was also a member of the American Sportsman Show Hall of Fame. He is survived by his wife Kay, 3 children, Charles, Amy and Randall, 5 grandchildren and 3 great grandchildren.